Managing Relationships

Managing
Relationships

Making a Life While Making a Living

JAGDISH PARIKH

CAPSTONE

Copyright © Jagdish Parikh 1999

The right of Jagdish Parikh to be identified as the author of this work has been asserted in accordance with the Copyright, Designs and Patents Act 1988

First published 1999 by
Capstone Publishing Limited (A Wiley Company)
8 Newtec Place
Magdalen Road
Oxford
OX4 1RE
United Kingdom
http://www.capstoneideas.com
email: info@wiley-capstone.co.uk

Reprinted 2001, 2002

British Library Cataloguing in Publication Data
A CIP catalogue record for this book is available from the British Library

ISBN 1-900961-18-0

Typeset in 10/13 pt Times by
Sparks Computer Solutions, Oxford
http://www.sparks.co.uk
Printed and bound by
T.J. International Ltd, Padstow, Cornwall

This book is printed on acid-free paper

Substantial discounts on bulk quantities of Capstone books are available to corporations, professional associations and other organizations. For details telephone Capstone Publishing on (+44-1865-798623) or fax (+44-1865-240941).

Dedicated to

Shaila

Prashant & Avani   Anuradha & Dev

Neal & Ishan

TABLE OF CONTENTS

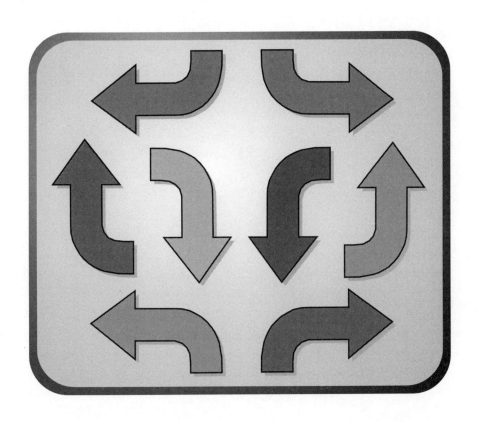

Managing relationships: understanding and enhancing life.

Acknowledgments

Over the years, I have met, heard and read many thinkers and authors. In this book, I have distilled concepts and processes relevant to the theme of this book from all that I have learnt from others, and integrated them in a manner that makes the approach to the issue of relationships profound as well as practical.

I remain indebted to all those innumerable sources which have influenced this book. It is really unfortunate that I am unable to individually identify and acknowledge their contributions.

Preface

This is a book with a difference to make a difference. It could be considered as a book of books. There are innumerable books that deal with a variety of topics included in this book. The difference is that this book has taken an overview – a helicopter view, so to speak – of most of the relevant issues and aspects that affect our lives and careers in the contemporary and emerging environment.

The focus is on the issue of *relationships*. In all dimensions of life – personal, professional and public – the key element, the ultimate competence that determines success or failure, happiness or distress, is the ability to manage one's relationships, within and without: with the inner dynamics within one's own self; and with the outer dynamics among people, things, events and ideas.

Obviously, to attempt writing about such a 'comprehensive' area is an almost impossible task. Even if one were to write a thorough and elaborate treatise on such a vast area, who would be able to read and absorb it? Yet it is becoming increasingly important and urgent for all of us who pursue active careers to become efficient and effective in our relationships all around, and achieve a sustainable balance between our personal and professional lives: *making a life while making a living.*

Keeping this in mind my approach has been twofold: to cover the entire topic in about 100 pages and in a style that is non-narrative, simple, clear and practical. This is perhaps running the risk of being too brief, which may be interpreted at times as not being deep enough as well as the opposite risk of making some material too dense. I have taken these risks in the hope that this material will give the reader at least a comprehensive conceptual framework of the mega issues confronting us today, along with some profound and basic, yet practical, suggestions and tools for becoming an effective leader of one's life and work.

Hopefully, this will enable one to shift from a fragmented world view which results in fractured and frustrated relationships, to a more integrated and professional life vision leading to more creative and meaningful relationships and lifestyles.

Jagdish Parikh

Introduction

The link between energy and matter ...
The bond between observer and observed ...
The interconnectedness of space and time ...
The unity of the fundamental forces
empowering the universe ...
Encountering these concepts from modern physics,
we nod in recognition.

In each of us, whatever our training, these terms resonate.
Intuitively, we know that they describe a great reality.
Early this century, physicist Albert Einstein
called this reality *relativity*.
In our own lives, we know and experience this reality
in the form of *relationships*.

Our whole life is relationships: a system of complex and ever-changing interconnections.

Our success and happiness are directly related to our ability to manage our relationships with people – at home, at work and elsewhere – as well as the full range of things, events, and ideas with which we interact.

Meaningful living is learning to create and sustain meaningful relationships all around us and in every respect. While this is a highly personal and subjective matter based on individual personalities and perceptions, some of the patterns and processes for forging relationships are universal. Once we understand some fundamentals of human nature and of the nature of relationships, we can use this understanding to build effective relationships.

For this, we need to cultivate insights about the *context* that surrounds relationships, the *structure* that informs them, and the *processes* that drive them. We can and should acquire and apply the requisite knowledge, skills and attitudes to manage all our relationships because, in doing so, we will find that we have forged the *missing link* to personal fulfillment.

This, in essence, is making a life while making a living.

THE CONTEXT: A NEW MIRROR

First, we must understand the ultimate context in which we manage our relationships, namely the *nature of reality* – our 'universe' and all its elements. Reality, we will discover upon some reflection, is much more 'dynamic' and 'interactive', and influenced by our perceptions much more than we may have realized.

Most of us have inherited (and reinforced through our formal schooling) a view of reality based on classical Newtonian physics. Newton's science was a beacon of light for his times, but his 'lengthened shadow', to quote Ralph Waldo Emerson, 'has blocked our vision, causing us to miss the potential brilliance of each passing day'.

Therefore, in order fully to appreciate life and its real scope and scale, we must become deeply 'aware' of and relate to reality, by understanding the tenets of the 'new physics' – for it is a much truer mirror of reality than the classical physics that has shaped our thinking. So, before turning to the subject of relationships, let us briefly tour the post-Newtonian world, to enable us to perceive and pursue this subject more deeply and meaningfully.

Modern physics began nearly a century ago, when Einstein first began to stare at the universe. In 1905, he published a paper on what he called a 'restricted principle of relativity'. In this paper he argued that energy and mass (or matter) are *different manifestations of the same reality*. In a sequel published in 1917, he offered an equation expressing the equivalence of energy and matter: the famous '$E = mc^2$': where E is energy, m is matter, and c is velocity.

For all of us, whatever our level of scientific training, the implications of Einstein's theory are inescapable. Einstein showed that *elements that seem very distinct, or unconnected or separate, may in fact be highly interconnected or related to one another* (in this example, energy and mass) *and may be highly interdependent.*

Over the past century, Einstein's fundamental discoveries about the profound relativity of the physical universe have led to many more findings – most recently and excitingly to a new theory, offered as a unified theory of all matter in the universe. Einstein believed that all matter was somehow unified, but he could only prove one aspect of this unification. His general theory of relativity only explained gravity, not the three other fields that make up the universe (the electromagnetic, the strong nuclear, and the weak nuclear forces – see Fig. 0.1). It was up to quantum mechanics to prove and establish unity in these fields.

Recently, the 'superstring' theory has helped to unite Einstein's theory of relativity to quantum physics, giving us one unified theory – the realization, in the words of physicist Michio Kaku of the City University of New York, that 'the four fundamental forces governing our universe are actually different manifestations of a single unifying force, governed by the superstring'.

According to Kaku, superstring theory challenges us to 'revise our understanding of the nature of matter'. From the days of the ancient Greeks until very recently, scientists have assumed that the universe is made up of tiny particles. Democritus called them *atomos*; we call them *atoms*. The superstring theory says that these particles contain something smaller – tiny strings, beyond the electrons, neutrons, protons, and even quarks, which make up 'everything from our bodies to the farthest star'. The strings move or vibrate, very much like the strings on a musical instrument. Matter consists of particles

Fig. 0.1   External physical forces.

that are different modes of vibration of the string. These particles are like musical notes. 'The "music" created by the string is matter itself', writes Kaku.

We will discuss this more elaborately in the concluding Part Three.

THE LIMITATIONS OF OUR CURRENT WORLD VIEW

So the universe is a symphony! How far this takes us from the confined world of the atom!

So the universe is a symphony! How far this takes us from the confined world of the atom! Classical physics is based on the assumption that 'to understand the whole, you must understand the parts', and this has resulted in analytical, mechanistic, deterministic, and reductionist thinking. No doubt, that classical view has enabled unprecedented and significant scientific and technological advances and material progress. In fact, in a sense, it has triggered the new physics. However, its limited and narrow view of reality has generated fragmented thinking and therefore distortion in our relationships, externally as well as within our selves.

The conventional view of reality based on classical physics has become outdated – not only by the advent of quantum physics, but also by the accelerating pace of change going on around us. The world we live in now is a universe away from the one that informed Newton's thinking 300 years ago. Revolutions – agricultural, industrial, technological and, most recently, informational – have dominated the past few centuries. There has been phenomenal intellectual, technological, and material progress. The magnitude and pace of change continue to grow, leading to overwhelming complexity, ongoing uncertainty and persistent conflict at many levels of our lives and relationships.

The lingering presence of a world view based on old science, combined with the rapid changes at the global level, has resulted in 'separatist' attitudes and therefore fractured relationships – not only with our environment but also within our own selves. To change this and cultivate more integrated and harmonious relationships within and around us, we must learn to think in terms of the cosmology of relationships. We must, in essence, create a 'unified theory' for our relationships – for our lives.

How can a unified theory of living change us as human beings – our perceptions of reality, our conception of ourselves, our values, our beliefs, our behavior, and our relationships?

Even a little reflection will show that the 'new physics' is very relevant in this regard, both conceptually and experientially. The new physics asserts that the ultimate reality is a complex web of interrelationships, an intricate system of self-organizing, autonomous subsystems of energy fields. Therefore, to understand any part, we must understand the whole, the larger systems of which it is a part. In this sense *everything is interrelated – a series of relationships within one vast relationship*. Managing even one single relationship requires a deeper appreciation of the fundamental nature and interconnectedness, a unified theory, of all relationships.

THE PARADOX OF SUCCESS

At the societal level, as measured by indices of scientific, technological and economic achievement, a significant segment of humanity is better off today than ever before. Consider the simple fact of life expectancy. In 1900, the

We must learn to think in terms of the cosmology of relationships.

Managing even one single relationship requires a deeper appreciation of the fundamental nature and interconnectedness of all relationships.

average life span of an individual living in a developed nation was less than 50 years; today it is closer to 80. The working week is shorter, pay is higher and consumer choice is broader.

Meanwhile, however, the human race seems to have *regressed* in many other ways. Every day we read of problems unheard of in our grandparents' generation: psychosomatic illnesses, murders, suicides committed by seemingly 'happy' people – the high-flying executive, the top level student, the model salesman, the rising politician and so on!

Of course, few of us become disturbed to the point of violence, but milder forms of negativity, such as chronic depression, have become very common in our society. Sales of mood-altering medications, such as the famous (or infamous) Prozac, keep rising – indicating a need for help just to accomplish the simple process of getting through a normal day: managing even the basic everyday relationships with people, things and events.

Why such anguish and anxiety? One possibility may be that as a consequence of the mass production and consumption system arising from the industrial and technological revolutions, the individual has become overspecialized and in a sense more 'standardized'. This weakens our individual sense of self worth and robs us of the ability to relate to ourselves and our surroundings appropriately.

Moreover, the global socioeconomic system, the growing power of mass media largely run by commercial interests and the absence of any significant inputs of enlightened values, either from the education system or family cultures, have led most individuals, especially in the developed countries (though developing countries are not far behind), to feel more alienated, 'disposable' and insecure.

So collectively and externally we may be doing well, but individually and internally many of us are doing poorly.

I describe this ironic situation as the 'paradox of success'. In the midst of unprecedented scientific and techno-economic achievements, we have a culture that is predominantly acquisitive and adversarial, and not at peace with itself – a condition of distorted relationships.

We have learned how to split the atom but not yet how to unite the world; we have learned how to reach the distant planets but not each other! We have been eminently successful in improving our *standard of living* at the material level, but we have failed to improve our *standard of life* at the experiential level.

Today, so-called good economics is often bad ethics and ecology – not to mention psychology – which goes to show that our 'standard of behavior' as measured by ethico-ecological indices has deteriorated. Essentially this means that our relationships with people, things, events and ideas have undermined our progress in some of the other dimensions of our lives.

A high standard of *living* implies better *things*; a high standard of *life* means better *thoughts and feelings*; a high standard of *behavior* means better *relationships* – *all these* leading to higher fulfillment and well-being. It is increasingly becoming clear that the purpose of life is not just to make a living. There is much more to life than just work, and there is much more to work than just work. We ask, 'Is that all there is?' That extra element – that 'more' that we

Collectively and externally we may be doing well, but individually and internally many of us are doing poorly.

We have learned how to split the atom but not yet how to unite the world; we have learned how to reach the distant planets but not each other!

are missing – lies in relationships. We can and must make a positive difference in our relationships.

A SEARCH FOR MEANING

At a personal or individual level, we need to make life more meaningful and fulfilling. We arrived in this world without being 'consulted' or even briefed as to why we are here or what is the purpose of our lives! Science and technology have given us many things to enhance our standard of living. We have acquired more money, power, position, prestige, etc., which are generally considered as elements of success. We pursue these elements of success, ultimately to feel 'good', feel satisfied, feel happy. But despite the increasing acquisition of these elements, most people have not experienced more happiness. In fact, many people admit that today they experience more frustration, fear, stress, conflict, disappointments, etc., than ever before! (See Fig. 0.2.)

Why is this so? Basically, there is nothing wrong or bad in these elements of success, namely money, power, position etc. The problem lies in the way we perceive and pursue these elements of success and relate to them. That is why, despite becoming 'successful' in the conventional sense, i.e. acquiring more and more money, power, prestige, etc in order to become proportionately 'happier', not only do most of us not seem to be happier, but, as observed earlier, most people seem to have more frustration, insecurity, conflict, and even fear at present than ever before! If this is so, then, we need to ask, 'Have we become more successful, or have we really become "successfools"?'

Have we become more successful, or have we really become "successfools"?

WHAT WE WANT	WHAT WE GET
(some examples)	(some examples)
◆ Success	◆ Frustration
◆ Achievement	◆ Stress
◆ Challenges	◆ Fun
◆ Power	◆ Conflicts
◆ Responsibility	◆ Time pressures
◆ Money	◆ Challenges
◆ Status	◆ Satisfaction
◆ Recognition	◆ Problems
◆ Health	◆ Friendships
◆ Family harmony	◆ Boredom

Fig. 0.2   Paradox of success: balance sheet of what we want and what we get.

We need to live a life that is not only 'successful', materially comfortable and secure, but which is also meaningful, truly fulfilling, satisfying, and 'happy'. What we really want is a more positive experience in life, i.e. more positive feelings – a result that can only come from a new way, a better way, of relating to life and its various elements.

However, we must also realize that these two dimensions, success and happiness, are entirely different aspects, and we commit a grave fallacy by assuming and expecting the two to be co-extensive: Success means *'getting what you want'* whereas happiness implies *'wanting what you get'*! We want both success as well as happiness in our life. The dilemma or challenge in life, therefore, is continuously to strive 'to get what we want', at the same time having the ability to experience the 'wanting of what we are getting' – and this, again, emphasizes the need for cultivating the ability to manage more effectively our multi-level and multi-dimensional relationships.

Success means 'getting what you want' whereas happiness implies 'wanting what you get'!

THE ANSWER: BETTER AND DEEPER RELATIONSHIPS

How can we raise these standards – of living and of life (becoming successful and happy) – and create a synthesis and even synergy between them? *How can we make a life while making a living?* For this we must identify what has led us into the present crisis, articulate the challenges at various levels of our lives, and propose some effective and practical suggestions for bringing about the desired changes in our lives – in our multifaceted relationships.

Central to achieving a deeper and more meaningful, successful and satisfying life is the need to build positive relations with people at the most immediate and intense level, and beyond that, with other people, things, events and ideas. We must recognize that relationships do not just happen. Considerable effort is required to cultivate authentic relationships and make them sustainable. Indeed, if all life is relationships, all the problems we face come from mismanaged relationships.

Why do we face this problem of mismanaged relationships?

One of Einstein's most frequently quoted statements is 'The problems we have today can never be solved at the level of thinking we were at when we created those problems'. And subsequently, with sadness, he states, 'With the splitting of the atom, with the advent of sub-atomic physics, everything has changed, save our level of thinking, and therefore we drift toward unparalleled disaster'. What is this different level of thinking that Einstein might be referring to? Probably, he refers to a level of thinking which is based on a deeper understanding of 'reality', and in that context with a higher level of awareness about one's self-identity and human relationships.

Unfortunately, most people do not think about what they are thinking about – and this is something to think about!

This implies that, in the emerging scenarios and in the context of rapid globalization of all relationships, it would be desirable to have an integrative level of thinking, a 'global' approach to develop a model of better and deeper relationships: integrating Western knowledge and Eastern wisdom – the 'scientific temper' of the West with the 'intuitive insights' of the East.

Towards this objective, this book offers some suggestions for synthesizing the technology of 'how to make a living', based on Western expertise, with the psychology of 'how to live', based on ideas in traditional Eastern philosophy.

Most people do not think abou what they are thinking about

This book synthesizes the technology of 'how to make c living', based on Western expertise, with the psychology of 'how to live' based on ideas in traditional Eastern philosophy.

The concepts in this book, however, are offered as neither a rebuttal nor a negation of religion or ideologies as a source of meaning and direction in human life. In fact, the concepts here are consistent with all the great contemporary and predominant creeds and belief systems. The ideas in this book should therefore be taken as supplementary to them, and not as a substitute.

The 'ism' here is not religious or political, it is practical: let us call it 'pragmatism' (not to be confused with the philosophical movement called 'pragmatism'). Such pragmatism, emphasizing harmonious relationships as the fundamental basis for human well-being and welfare, could become an important enabling 'ism' for our future. This book has attempted as comprehensive and integrative an approach and as relevant, effective and harmonizing a framework of 'perception and connection' as possible, to serve as an infrastructure for all levels and dimensions of relationships: *providing the missing link for making a life while making a living.*

With that in mind, in the following pages, a pragmatic perspective will guide us as we explore:

◆ **definition of relationships** (the 'what') – Part One

◆ **dynamics of relationships** (the 'why') – Part Two

◆ **deepening relationships** (the 'how') – Part Three.

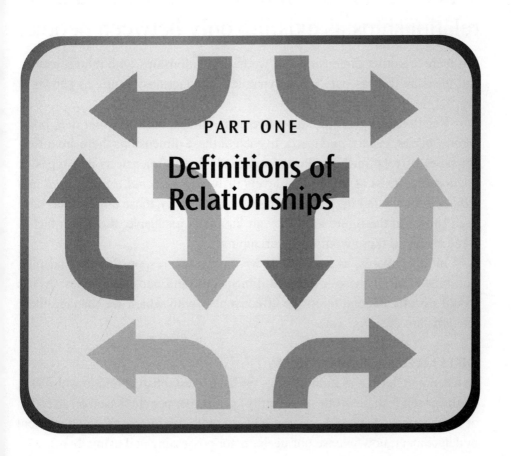

PART ONE

Definitions of Relationships

What is a relationship? Generally we think of relationships as existing only between people.

But there are other dimensions, as we have relationships with things, events, and ideas as well as our 'inner dynamics' or innermost 'self', as shown in Fig. 1.1.

Relationships therefore have five main dimensions: *the inner Self, other people, things, events, and ideas.* In each of these dimensions there are different types of relationships. Furthermore, all these dimensions and types of relationships exist at three main levels of living: *personal, professional and public*, as shown in Fig. 1.2. For the sake of simplicity, these three arenas have been shown in the figure as if they are mutually exclusive, though in fact to some extent all these would be overlapping.

In other words, as individuals we have roles, responsibilities and relationships at all of these levels and dimensions, and our effectiveness in life would directly depend upon the effectiveness with which we manage these relationships (see Fig. 1.3).

THREE LEVELS OF RELATIONSHIPS

At a *personal* level – as individuals – we have to establish a 'relationship' with our inner self (establish our self identity), with other people (based on affection or expectations; roles and responsibilities), with things (based on attachment or detachment; how intense our desire is for possessing and using them), with

Fig. 1.1   Relationships.

	DIMENSIONS				
LEVELS	*Inner Self*	*People*	*Things*	*Events*	*Ideas*
Personal					
Professional					
Public					

Fig. 1.2   Matrix of levels and dimensions of relationships.

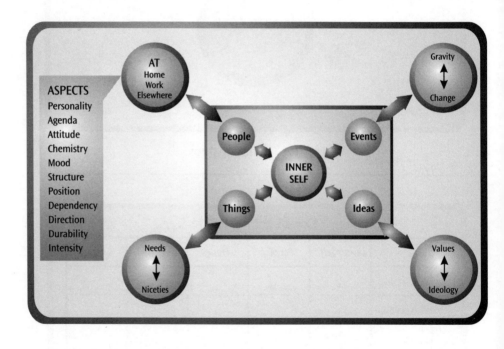

Fig. 1.3   The framework of relationships: the arena of life.

events (based on reactivity or proactivity; how we respond to situations) and with ideas (our beliefs, biases, prejudices, etc.).

Similarly, at the *professional* level, i.e. as a manager, how we relate to our inner Self (while working, what is our inner 'reference point'), how do we relate to other people (superiors, peers, subordinates, etc., at the workplace), and with various things, events, and ideas relevant at this level.

At the *public* level, or in our public life, the manner in which we relate to the various entities in the community will determine whether we experience and generate conflict or harmony.

We will now examine some aspects of relationships at these three levels with regard to each of the five dimensions mentioned above (Fig. 1.2).

PERSONAL LEVEL

Relationship with inner self
All our relationships begin within. One needs to be able to relate to oneself – or shall we say one's Self – effectively before relating to anything or anyone else.

What is the self? Until someone asks, we seem to know. When we want to explain, we do not know – we fumble! If we were asked who or what it is that we are referring to when we use the word 'I', what would we say? Most people find this a rather difficult and even uncomfortable question. It seems beyond intellectual comprehension and verbal articulation.

What is self? Until someone asks, we seem to know. When we want to explain, we do not know!

Clearly, we are not merely the name we carry. That is just a label given to us at birth by others. Even if we change it to a preferred name, we – our 'Self' – still would continue to be the same. The primary implication of a name is that it is a word or sound used by others to identify us.

If one has to describe, even in detail, the organization in which one has been working for a few years, it would be relatively easy to do so; but when it comes to describing one's inner self, the 'organization' inside one's skin with which one has been living all one's life, even the most articulate person will find it difficult!

Generally, however, one identifies one's self with one's name or one's thinking, values, experiences, roles, relationships, status, feelings and so on; and, of course, one's body. To put it rather more simply, one usually identifies with one's body, mind and emotions. Now let us explore this notion and examine whether this identity is valid to gain a better understanding of what the self really is and what it is not, and how to relate to it.

Let us consider this dialogue: if I ask you, 'Whose shirt are you wearing?' you would say, 'It is my shirt'. That implies that you are the owner, user, and experiencer of your shirt. You are thereby also implying that you are not the shirt: this is *your* shirt – you *have* a shirt. In other words, whatever is yours is not you, almost by definition. The owner (the subject) and the owned (the object) are separate.

Pursuing this further, if I ask you 'Whose body is this on which you are wearing this shirt?' your response would naturally be, 'It is my body'. This would indicate that you *have* a body (in a sense, just as you *have* a shirt) but that you *are not* the body. There is something inside the body which says 'This is my body' – indicating that it is separate from the body. Now, if I ask you if you are experiencing some thoughts, you would say yes. Suppose I ask you: 'Whose thoughts are those, the ones you are now experiencing?' you would again say 'mine'. Just as you are not your shirt or your body, you are also not your thoughts, i.e. not your thinking or your mind. Thoughts come and go, they change, but you, the 'owner', the experiencer of those thoughts, are always there! In other words, you are the owner, the manager, the experiencer, or observer of your body and mind. But if you are neither your body nor your mind, then what or who are you?

This question might generate some uncomfortable feeling, and so now I ask, 'Whose feeling is that?' Obviously, you would say 'mine'. Again, you *have* feelings, but you *are not* your feelings.

You have feelings, but you are not your feelings.

Your anger, fear, frustration, guilt, jealousy or regret might seem intensely personalized – yet these emotions are not you. You are the owner, experiencer of all these feelings. Feelings come and go, they keep changing, but you are always there.

In the same way, you are also not your name – you *have* a name. You can change your name any time, your name tag will change, but you do not cease to exist! You will simply be known by another name.

By now you could be feeling exasperated. You might say 'I realize that I am not my body, my thoughts, or my mind, nor even my feelings. But then what is left of me? What am I?'

My final question then would be 'Have you changed in the last few years?'

You might say 'Yes. My body has changed and so have my mind and my emotions.' My response would then be 'In other words, all that you *have* has changed. But who or what, inside your skin, knows or is aware that all these have changed?' At this point you might discover that throughout your life you have had within you an abiding constant awareness or consciousness, which has been a kind of constant witness to your life – to all that you considered as your self. It is this witness – this awareness or consciousness – that is the real you: the 'I' who knows 'you'.

It is this awareness or consciousness that is the real you: the 'I' who knows 'you'.

In summary, you *have* a body, mind, and emotions, but in deeper reality you *are* none of these. Of course, all these are an integral, unique and inseparable 'parts' of you, and collectively they constitute what is generally described as your 'ego-self'. They could be considered as the *functional areas of your self* and you should relate to them as such, as shown in Fig. 1.4. Your true self is that who or which is conscious of these other parts – the inner dynamics – which should be recognized as the 'ego self'.

Relationships with other people

Relationships with others can be with individuals or with groups. The following section sketches very briefly some basic issues in our relationships with people at different levels, indicating a 'key issue' that may make or break any relationship. Later we will see how our attitudes can play a critical role in the creation and sustenance of our relationships.

There are mainly six types of relationship at this level.

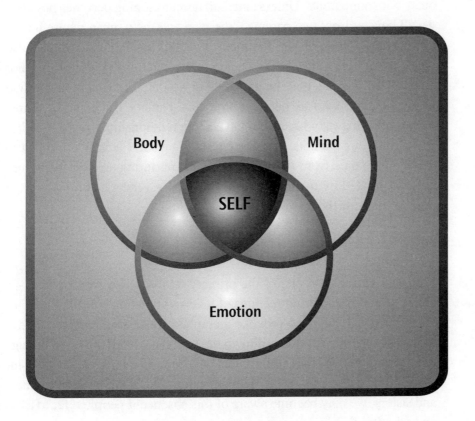

Fig. 1.4   The real Self.

1   **Parents**. The earliest and therefore most primary relationship is obviously with our parents. Unless and until human cloning becomes possible, we all have at least two parents – the man and the woman whose union, however brief, gave us life. For most of us, this man and this woman also raised us, adding a deeper dimension to our relationship with them. For others, birth parents may be unknown or absent. Their relationship will be to caregivers who are not their biological parents. But however simple or complex that may be, we all have some relationship – present and/or past – with our 'parents'. During our early years, it is very important to receive guidance from them through their nurturing without being unduly dominated by them. Key issue: *nurturing* versus *control* (from the point of view of the receiver).

In addition, we may have relationships with the following:

2   **Siblings**. This is also one of the primary relationships we can have – a connection that can bring feelings of love and bonding ('brotherhood' or 'sisterhood'). It can also provoke a competitive instinct – hence the famous 'sibling rivalry'. According to the famed birth order theory, our age relationship to our other siblings can determine our outlook, as the 'oldest', the 'middle child' or the 'baby' for example. If we have no brothers and sisters, we may become aware of this absence if people refer to us as an 'only child'. Key issue: *bonding* versus *competition*.

3   **Children**. Again, this is a fundamental relationship. To have a child is to have an opportunity to love, guide, and let go. This is the positive side of parenting. The negative side is a tendency to live through our children. Key issue: *nurturing* versus *control* (from the point of view of the giver).

4   **Extended family**. By definition this relationship comes through a connecting person. If we have a grandparent, an uncle or aunt, or a cousin, we are connected to this 'relative' through our relationship with a parent. Therefore, always by definition, the relationship is triangular. In many cases, we might compare the relative to someone in our family. We might compare our uncle to our father, our aunt to our mother, or our cousin to a sibling. If the comparison is favorable to the relative, this can bring solace (by giving and receiving needed support, for example) or it can bring resentment (because of absence of support from the primary family member). Key issue: *positive/negative comparison.*

5   **Spouse**. This is another primary relationship – considered absolutely primal in some cultures. One says 'my other half' or even 'my better half'. Through the legal process (and, in some religions, through holy sacrament) of marriage, two people become one. The desire for physical (sexual) union that often motivates marriage is a clear sign of this theme. On a more mundane material level, marriage may bring unity of possessions – as, for example, with possessions that are considered to be owned jointly in communal property jurisdictions – or it may be in a spiritual sense – as

when the biblical heroine Ruth said to her husband 'Wherever you go, I will go, and your people will become my people and your God will become my God'. Such statements express not only the commitment but also the complexity of marriage – which is not only to a person but to all the relationships of that person, including the person's family (in-laws). Key issue: *presence or absence of unity* with the spouse and the spouse's family.

6   **Friends**. The connection between two friends is considered to be extremely important – indeed fundamental – to human happiness. A friendship can be as close and as lasting as a tie by family or marriage. Friends communicate, enjoy common activities and support one another. Although it is possible to go through periods of our lives without a close friend, it is rare to go through a lifetime without any. Key issue: *sharing/support.*

In the above examples, we had a glimpse of six common types of personal relationships that most people have. Now let us consider the fact that *all of the above relationships are closely interconnected.* Our relationship with our parents affects our relationships with our siblings, children, extended family, and spouse. For example, one cause of sibling rivalry is competition for the affection of one or both parents. As another example, if our parents fought a lot when we were growing up, we are likely to have this tendency ourselves in relation to our spouse (or work on resisting it). So this means that each of the six relationships mentioned has the potential for a multiplier effect – and so far we have considered this merely at the personal level – not to mention the possible multipliers at the professional and public levels!

Aspects of relationships

The dynamics of each relationship between people would depend upon the specific 'situation' or profile of that relationship. Given below are some examples of these profiles using one-on-one relationships for the purpose of brevity and simplicity (see Fig. 1.3: Aspects).

◆ **Personality**. There are many ways to analyze personality traits, ranging from sophisticated models such as the Myers–Briggs personality types (extrovert/introvert, sensing/intuitive, thinking/feeling, judging/perceiving) or dominance models, skill assessment, etc., to just simple concepts such as 'nice' or 'friendly', 'arrogant', 'adversarial', 'genius', 'stupid', and so on. The interaction, the dynamics, in any relationship, would be significantly influenced by the 'personalities' involved.

◆ **Agenda**. A relationship may or may not have a known agenda or plan. This plan may be in the mind of one or both parties. It may be open or hidden; positive or negative.

◆ **Attitude**. A relationship can be shaded by the attitude we bring toward the other person: positive, negative, or neutral; caring or critical; selfish or supportive.

◆ **Chemistry**. In any given relationship, there is a bond between people, commonly referred to as 'chemistry'. This bond can give us a variety of feelings, but they broadly fall into three categories: attraction, repulsion, or indifference. In reality, one can perceive a whole spectrum of 'chemistries' between attraction and repulsion.

◆ **Mood**. People's moods generally do not remain constant. At any given moment in time, the people in a relationship may be experiencing sadness or happiness – positive or negative feelings – which will color their interaction. More complex emotional states such as anger (or acceptance) and fear (or trust) may also affect an interaction.

◆ **Structure**. Relationships with other people may possess a certain structure, such as 'workplace' or 'home'. This structure will define certain boundaries of the relationship.

◆ **Position**. A person may be our superior, our peer, or our subordinate at work, at home, or elsewhere in the community. The dynamics of any relationship would be influenced by the relative positions of the persons interacting.

◆ **Dependency**. The people involved in relationships may be described as dependent, independent, or interdependent, based on how much need they feel they have for each other.

◆ **Direction**. Relationships often are moving, either becoming closer or more distant with time.

◆ **Durability**. Relationships may be permanent or temporary.

◆ **Intensity**. The feelings evoked by a relationship may be strong or weak, and this would naturally color the relationship.

We could sense from the above discussed variety of the factors and situations that affect the dynamics of any relationship, that relationship between people is one of the most complex, delicate and deep elements in one's life. For most people, this dimension of relationship is also the most critical in determining one's experience of life – positive or negative. It is therefore of utmost importance that we become aware of, understand and cultivate the ability to 'manage' this dimension effectively. A basic approach to this is discussed more elaborately in Parts Two and Three.

Relationships with things
In addition to our relationship with our self and with others, we have relationships with things in terms of our desire or otherwise for them. We want to own, enjoy, or consume a variety of things. Everyone has such desires. But all desires are not of the same kind or intensity.

In order to simplify our relationship with things, we can classify desires for them into two basic categories.

◆ There are things that we truly *need*, i.e. we must have them for sheer survival. Therefore, by our very definition of a 'need', any nonfulfillment of a 'need' is a real disaster.

◆ All other desires for various things that are not essential for survival are wishes or 'wants', or we might say 'niceties'. Nice to have them, but the nonfulfillment of a nicety, though it may cause some disappointment or sadness, is not a disaster.

The distinction between 'need' and 'nicety' is based on how we relate to their loss: is it disaster or disappointment? In that sense, needs are primary, whereas niceties are secondary. As shown in Fig. 1.5, our real needs at all levels – physical, social, psychological – are very few indeed.

The distinction between 'need' and 'nicety' is how we relate to their loss: is it disaster or disappointment?

Things such as food, fresh air, water and shelter are 'needs' at the *physiological* survival level. These needs must be fulfilled; our lives depend on them. Similarly, at the *sociological, affiliation* or *emotional* level as well as the *psychological* achievement and *self-worth* level, we, as human beings, need a few things. For our emotional as well as psychological survival, we need some tangible modicum of nurturing in our youth, some degree of affiliation and some measurable success and recognition in our adulthood, and caring in our older age (see Fig. 1.5).

All the other things we desire or *want* –our niceties – are secondary. We may desire these things, but they are not essential for our existence. They may be good to have but they are not vital for our survival. In fact, beyond a point,

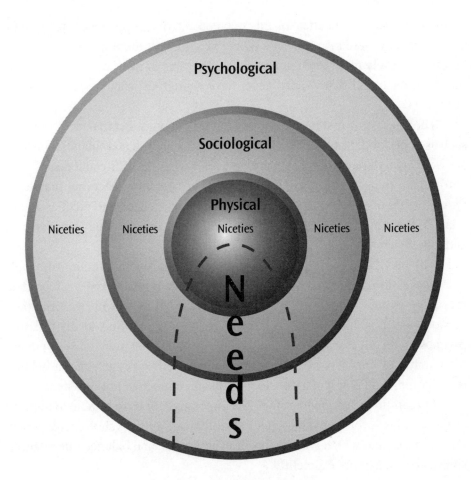

Fig. 1.5   Needs and niceties.

excessive pursuit of 'niceties' results in greed and overdependence, relating to them as if they were also 'needs'. When we don't get them we overreact and become intensely frustrated than would be desirable or justified. Moreover, we should never forget that we can never have enough of what we really do not need!

We can never have enough of what we really do not need!

The interesting and important thing to reflect on is that material comforts such as good food, fashionable clothing, luxurious house and financial fortune are wonderful things to have, but are they really matters of life and death? The unfortunate thing is that most of us forget, or somehow become unable, to remain aware of or recognize this distinction between need and niceties and to relate to them as such. Generally, therefore, we have a tendency to overreact and thereby contaminate our experience of life.

The inevitable consequence is that there is a growing amount of avoidable depression almost universally in our overly consumerist society. The prevailing culture of measuring 'success' primarily in terms of 'material possessions and positions' has accelerated frustrations, leading to distress and psychosomatic illnesses. The situation in business is even more tense – witness the number of conflicts and suicides over what a healthy psyche, a healthy relationship, would at worst consider as disappointments, not disasters.

On careful reflection therefore it is imperative for us to be able to identify at the various levels (physiological, sociological, and psychological) which are our needs and which are niceties or even greeds, and balance our relationship with things more efficiently.

Let us now explore this theme as we look at some of the 'things' with which we have strong relationships – some needs and some niceties.

◆ **Food**. This of course is a basic need. Without it, we die. Beyond this, when it gets into the 'nicety' category, food can and does assume additional significance. It can become the vehicle for group gatherings (the proverbial 'family dinner'), for courtship ('candlelit dinner'), and for business dealings ('power breakfast'). Because of its importance both in terms of survival and social integration, food becomes a ready symbol for other elements. However, if one's dependence on food goes beyond a moderate level, one may develop eating disorders that may indicate undesirable attitudes and an unhealthy relationship with food. Cultivating a healthy relationship with food implies disciplining and balancing our diet in terms of quantity and quality. Key issues: *survival, integration, health.*

◆ **Clothing**. A certain amount of clothing to protect us from the elements is absolutely necessary and to that extent it is a need. But do clothes 'make the man'? Not quite, though clothes are intrinsic to human beings. Clothing, of course, has far more than a utilitarian purpose – the outfits we wear do more than protect us against the elements. On the most fundamental level, they provide us with a basic level of personal modesty. Although this level may range from low (in Saint Tropez) to high (in Tehran), it is a fundamental value in all cultures. Beyond the function of modesty, clothes have a purpose of integration into events. Many occasions, such as business, parties and worship, require a certain style of dressing and our ability to dress suitably for such occasions can become a ticket to acceptance. Clothes may ease our ongoing acceptance into certain groups – from punk rock to pinstripe. Finally, clothes may be a vehicle for personal expression (usually within the confines of an event or group). The energy and resources that we expend in building our wardrobes, in these senses, gives us a relationship to our clothing. Key issues: *modesty, acceptance, expression.*

◆ **Home**. The most important building of course is the place we live, our domicile – or, to use a more emotionally loaded term, our home. At the physiological 'need' level, our homes shelter us from the natural elements. At the psychological and sociological level, our homes provide us with some measure of security and stability. Popular culture offers many expressions on the importance of the home – 'There's no place like home', 'Home is where the heart is', 'Home sweet home'. One has also to remember that a beautiful house by itself does not necessarily ensure a happy home! Our homes and their furnishings may also reflect our economic status, our tastes and even our personalities. Key issues: *shelter, security, stability, status, responsibility.*

A beautiful house by itself does not necessarily ensure a happy home!

◆ **Alcohol**. Do we need alcohol? No. Yet some people develop a dependency on this addictive substance. This is truly a case where something that once was a 'want' – a 'nicety' – begins to masquerade as a 'need' and addiction sets in. Alcoholics in their addiction have been known to call alcohol their 'best friend' – a primary relationship indeed! Cigarettes, nonmedicinal drugs and sometimes even chewing gum can also be addictive – to virtually anyone. Key issue: *potential for addiction.*

◆ **Cars**. It might seem strange to suggest that we can have a 'relationship' with an automobile, and yet we can. Its very name suggests autonomy and mobility, obviously important goals. Our cars, an important 'nicety', often reflect our economic status, our stage in life, our tastes, and even our personalities. By itself, there is nothing undesirable in enjoying the possession and use of an impressive car – as long as there is no overdependence on it. It is certainly not a basic need for survival. For any reason, if we are dispossessed of that car, temporarily or even permanently, of course it would cause discomfort and inconvenience, but it should not cause us a feeling of disaster – our survival is not threatened. Key issues: *mobility, expression, responsibility.*

Relationships with events
Our relationships with our own selves, with people, and with things, coexist with our relationship with events.

When we face an event, quite often, there is a gap between our *expectations* of the event and what we actually get from it, our *achievement*. There is also another kind of gap and that is between our *intention* to act or behave in a certain way, and our actual *action* or behavior.

To relate to any event in an appropriate way, it would be very helpful for us to classify events into either changeable or non-changeable.

Whenever there is such a perceived gap, we could relate to the event either in a reactive or a proactive way. To relate to any event in an appropriate way, it would be very helpful for us to classify events into either changeable or non-changeable. We could describe the non-changeable events as 'gravities'.

For example, there is gravity in our planet Earth: it limits and regulates our life significantly, and yet we do not complain against it! Why not? The reason is that we have accepted gravity as a totally unchangeable fact of life.

Similarly, there are many things and situations in life with the same character of non-changeability similar to that of gravity, either permanently or at least for a specific period of time. Such non-changeabilities or gravities pervade in our lives at all levels: individual, organizational and societal (see Fig. 1.6).

For example, at the individual or personal level, there are several physical aspects, or features of our body, that cannot be changed during our entire life, and some (for example, weight) that are non-changeable for a specific period. Moreover, there are similar 'gravities' in other dimensions of our mental and emotional self, either permanently or for a specific period of time.

The same analyses apply to the organizational and societal levels as well. We do become agitated quite frequently over situations or things that are un-changeable, at least for a period. We fritter away our precious and limited time, energy, and resources in trying to change such 'gravities'. Obviously, there are several situations and things which could be influenced and changed, but if our attention and energies are engaged in fighting against gravities, the effective-ness of our efforts to change things and situations in other areas would be limited and seriously adversely affected.

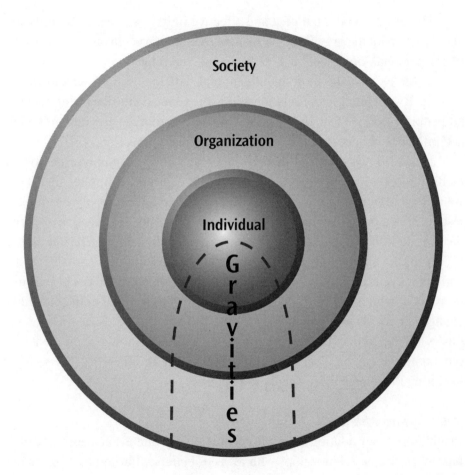

Fig. 1.6   Gravities.

Therefore, to be intelligent and effective in life, we need to identify explicitly what are the gravities – permanent or temporary – in our lives at all the levels, personal, organizational, and societal, and relate to them as such. This will enable us to make more intelligent and judicious use of our limited resources. By positioning our relationship with events in this manner and setting proper priorities, we can, over a period, not only minimize gravities around us and influence change, but also minimize our frustrations.

We need to identify explicitly what are the gravities – permanent or temporary – in our lives at all the levels.

It must be emphasized that this approach does not imply a passive or fatalistic acceptance of everything. Quite the contrary. It implies that if we want to be effective in our 'change' strategies, we have to apply our limited resources in a proactive and creative manner, free from any reactive or prejudiced attitude, and not dissipating them in a dysfunctional way. The one crucial aspect in this approach is to be honest and objective in our assessment of a particular event as gravity or a changeability. However, there could be situations about which we may not be able to judge clearly whether they could be changed or not. That is why in Fig. 1.6 the dividing line between gravities and others is a dotted line. In such situations, our approach should be on a tentative basis until we can be clear about its changeability or otherwise. We shall be exploring this theme more deeply in Part Two.

Relationships with ideas

In addition to our relationships with people, things and events, each one of us has, in a sense, a 'relationship' with ideas or beliefs – our mindsets or mental models – the perceptual filters through which we perceive and experience life.

In fact, this is a basic relationship which affects all of our other relationships. Our very perceptions of, and therefore our relationships with, our Self, people, things and events depend upon our ideas and beliefs. Our beliefs determine our behavior and our experiences.

Our beliefs determine our behavior and our experiences.

Each person has unique ideas, belief system and attitudes, depending upon several variables such as childhood upbringing and experiences, education, media exposure, friends, profession, etc. Every individual would have beliefs referring to issues at various levels – personal, professional and public – which would determine that person's relationships at those levels.

However, there are some ideas or beliefs that are fundamental, somewhat like an infrastructure on which the superstructure of all other ideas and beliefs depends at various levels. These fundamental ideas would be about some of the existential issues that would influence one's choices of values, religion, political ideology, and so on.

The critical existential issues are *freedom, isolation, death,* and above all (or shall we say beneath all) is the issue of the *meaning and purpose of life.* We shall revisit these issues in depth in the concluding Part Three.

When ideas are collectively shared, they become 'isms'—belief systems based on collectively shared values. All throughout history, there have been several 'isms' or ideologies expressing social, economic, political, ethical and religious ideas. Several have been advocated and practised in different parts of the world during this century with varying degrees of success (or failure).

These 'isms', belief systems or ideas, in fact, represent different combinations of two basic parameters: *values* and *ideologies*. A good example of a value extreme would be spiritualism versus materialism – the old idea that we 'cannot serve two masters', namely God and money! Ideology extremes are individual-focused (freedom or conflict at one extreme) versus collective-focused (community welfare or command society at the other extreme).

As shown in Fig. 1.7, the 'value-laden' A–B axis covers the whole spectrum of values, ranging from the spiritual (emphasized in Eastern cultures) to the materialistic (dominant in contemporary Western thinking and, perhaps, now dominating everywhere) – that is, in a sense, ranging from a self-denying to a self-centered approach. History has shown that neither becoming totally spiritual nor remaining intensely materialistic, nor any compromises in between, bring about the kind of meaning and richness that one should and can achieve in one's life.

If becoming absolutely spiritual implies withdrawal from the 'material' world, from the activities of the world, then it would imply denying our 'self', a kind of escape from the experiences of active and dynamic life – becoming 'selfless'. On the other hand, becoming totally absorbed in the material world could make us ego-centered, self-centered, or selfish. Both these extremes are undesirable and so are any 'compromises' in between … as these would lead to a suboptimal living.

The 'ideology' C–D axis covers a different range of ideological stances. These range from freedom of the individual on the one hand, to a complete integration with society on the other; that is, ranging from competition to collectivism, or from capitalism to communism.

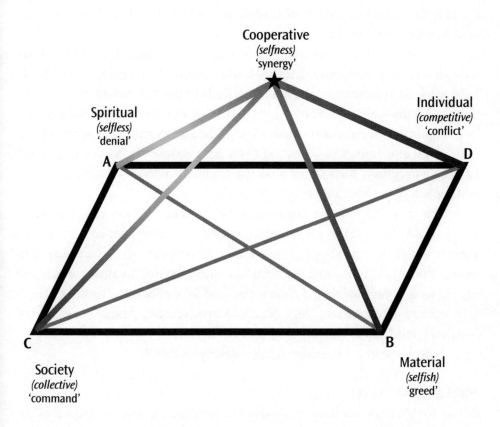

Fig. 1.7   The values–ideology axis: the human challenge.

While full freedom of the individual is desirable for the blossoming of the individual, unrestricted or undisciplined freedom for all individuals could lead to chaos and conflict. Today, we are witnessing in some so-called 'free societies', despite some regulatory constraints, that undisciplined freedom has led to adversarial competition, a win–lose conflict-ridden environment. Similarly, at the other extreme, we have also noticed in case of the totalitarian regimes such as communism, as was practiced in the Soviet Union, that it had resulted in a 'command' society and smothering of the individual. As is well known, none of these extremes or 'isms', nor any compromises in between, have yet been able to achieve their stated objectives, namely individual welfare or societal growth on an equitable or durable basis.

The ideal relationship, the meaningful balance between values and ideology, would be to achieve a synthesis, a kind of synergy, between these two parameters, as shown in Fig,1.7: functioning in the material roles and activities in our life, while remaining anchored in strong spiritual values, which can enable us to contribute to and enhance individual wellbeing as well as collective welfare – functioning with detached involvement, neither 'selfish' nor 'selfless', but from a dynamic synthesis of 'Selfness'.

This theme is also discussed more deeply in Part 3.

PROFESSIONAL LEVEL

So far we have considered relationships at the personal level with each of the five dimensions – inner self, people, things, events, and ideas (see Fig. 1.2).

Now, we will consider relationships at the professional level, as a manager, mainly within the context of an organization.

Relationship with the inner self
One's behavior and performance at work with other people, things, events and ideas, will be reactive or proactive, depending on what identity, what relationship one keeps with one's inner self. If one identifies with one's ego-Self, as discussed earlier, one will function more in a reactive, fight–flight mode. Whereas if one remains in the consciousness of one's inner Self, as the 'internal reference point' – Self-reference – one will be able to relate to everyone and everything more proactively, and thereby cultivate more authentic, durable, and harmonious relationships all around: neither being 'selfish' nor 'selfless', but functioning with 'Selfness'.

Relationship with other people
Keeping the context of the organization, most importantly there would be the following types of relationships:

◆ **Relationships between superiors and subordinates**. Most people at work have a superior – someone who guides and monitors their performance – and many people themselves function as superiors – guiding and monitoring the performance of others. Inevitably, the upstream relationship affects the downstream relationship, as managers are affected by the style of their bosses, which influences their own styles as bosses. Whether the relationship is upstream or downstream a common concern is whether the boss is empowering the subordinate or merely wielding power over the subordinate, and whether the subordinate is cooperative and responsive. Key theme: use/abuse of *power/support/cooperation*.

◆ **Relationships with peers/colleagues/co-workers**. In most work settings, employees have co-workers. To a greater or lesser degree, their performance and sense of fulfillment depend on their relationships with their co-workers, as their work is quite often interdependent. For example, one might be in a job that generates revenue and the other might be responsible for monitoring it; or they may work in the same function – for example, they both might be working in a team on the same project. In either situation, it would be critical for each of them to have an appropriate relationship with each other in the interests of ensuring their performance and achieving their objectives.

Team building exercises by themselves are not likely to create the deeply and ndividually felt group synergy'.

The contemporary rising emphasis on 'management by teams' and team building processes, is indicative of the importance of establishing suitable attitudes and relationships at all levels within the organization. However, while the various indoor or outdoor team building exercises are refreshing and useful, by themselves they are not likely to create the deeply and individually felt 'group synergy' that is essential for authentic and durable team work.

It should be borne in mind that effectiveness in the relationship not only depends on the work-related relationship, but in fact, the work-related relationship itself will depend on the deeper level of person-to-person relationship. This is often overlooked. Therefore there is a lot of avoidable frustration because efforts focused mainly on the work-related relationship have not only not forged authentic relationships but, frequently, have led to manipulative and artificial relationships. Witness the persisting lack of mutual trust among workers at all levels despite the growing number of 'team-building' training sessions! That is not to say that such efforts or processes are undesirable – the point here is that these do not go far enough. Ultimately, any relationship will begin and depend on one's own relationship with all the 'dimensions' at the personal level – and this is the main missing link. Key issue: presence or absence of *trust/support/teamwork.*

◆ **Relationships with customers**. Whether one is involved, directly or indirectly, in selling a product or service, whether for profit or otherwise, it is almost an axiom that unless the customer expectations are fulfilled, the relationship with the customer is not likely to survive for long. With increasing competitive pressures, it is imperative for every organization to ensure that the customer is the driving force for its (and therefore its managers') activities. In fact, now it is not enough to just fulfill customer expectations; it has become a survival issue for any organization to ensure not only 'customer delight', but to achieve 'customer loyalty' – a deeper and more durable relationship. Key issues: *quality/price/service* (from the standpoint of the provider).

◆ **Relationships with suppliers**. It is also obvious that the ultimate quality, price and dependability of any product or service naturally depends on the quality, price and dependability of the material and service you get from your suppliers – and one of the major forces that can ensure all these at a satisfactory level is of course an ongoing and effective relationship with suppliers. Key issues: *quality/price/service* (from the standpoint of the receiver).

◆ **Relationships with competitors**. This might not seem like a 'relationship', but it is one, and an important one. Moreover it can be, and as far as possible one should try to make it, a positive one. Even if a company has a unique product with a unique niche, a major market share and a dominant position in the market, sooner or later (usually sooner) competitors will arrive. With proper insight and foresight, and a deliberate effort, it would be in the interest of any company to keep an appropriate level of contacts and relationships with competitors. The significance of this relationship can be gauged from the increasing number of strategic alliances, acquisitions and mergers. Key issues: *cooperative competition*.

◆ **Relationships with community**. No matter how intangible its products or services may be, any profession or business operates in the context of a community – local, regional, national and/or international. This relationship extends beyond one's primary relationships with superiors, subordinates, peers, customers, suppliers and competitors. The community 'supplies' the infrastructure, land, people and utilities. Any profession or business, in turn, 'supplies' employment, goods and services and contributes taxes.

In the process of this 'exchange', there are quite often interfaces that can generate 'conflicts of interests'. What may be good economics for a profession or business may turn out to be bad ethics or ecology, or both – and vice versa. This is a very basic issue and is becoming increasingly critical and visible: how can one 'relate' to these issues effectively and achieve an ongoing balance among economics, ethics and ecology. Key issues: *balancing economics, ethics and ecology.*

What may be good economics for a profession or business may turn out to be bad ethics or ecology, or both – and vice versa.

Relationship with things

Until recently, many types of work depended very heavily on things. Humankind has relied on physical tools from the Stone Age to the present era. In fact, until recent years, every profession has had some physical tool as the emblem of its craft. Paraphrasing from 'Vanished Work', by the German poet Hans Magnus Enzenberger, we collectively feel the loss of the need of the rushman, the hive of the beekeeper, the flue of the charcoal burner, the teasel of the woolcarder, and the chisel of the trough-maker!

With the advent of the Industrial Age and then the Information Age, this closeness to tools began to wane. 'What has happened to the bridoons, the hames and the turrets? The cartwright has passed away. Only his name survives, like an insect congealed in amber, in the telephone book', writes Enzenberger.

Yet despite the passing of crafts and tools, we still have the implements of our professions and trade. These *things* are less personal than the tools of trade in days gone by, but even today the importance and significance of *things* in our work lives should not be underestimated.

In the earlier days the professional tools and *things* that were needed and used were unique and remained relatively unchanged for long periods of time. In the contemporary situation, however, with the accelerating pace of technological change, the tools and *things* – the hardware and the software – we use are constantly changing. The key issue in this regard is the intensifying need to cultivate psychological alertness and flexibility as well as technological skills to keep updated with the 'state of the art' in one's profession.

Relationship with events
The issues in this regard are similar to those considered at the personal level (Fig. 1.6). Firstly, dealing with the gap between one's expectations and actual achievement from any specific event. Secondly, coping with the events that are not changeable for a specific period of time and cultivating the relevant competencies for proactively bringing about the desired change in the events and situations that are considered as changeable. As mentioned earlier, this will be discussed in depth in Part Two.

Relationship with ideas
At a personal level, our relationship with ideas is along the values–ideology axis (Fig. 1.7), ranging between the spiritual and materialistic on the one hand,

and between individual interests and the community interests on the other. At the professional level, the issue of relationship with ideas would be primarily concerned with one's professional interests, expertise, and activities.

It is imperative that in the contemporary scenarios of accelerating change and intensifying competition, any professional, to achieve a sustainable superiority, or at least a sustainable success, will have to have an intellectual agility and flexibility, to keep updated with the latest ideas and trends, at the global level in general, and in one's professional area in particular. Intelligence by itself is no longer enough – expertise and relevance are essential.

Intelligence by itself is no longer enough – expertise and relevance are essential.

In this context, creativity and innovation assume primary importance. But the concept of creativity needs to be revisited. Most of the contemporary literature, conferences and seminars are focused on 'intellectual' creativity. This is of course important and necessary, but no longer enough.

What is now becoming increasingly essential, in this era of overwhelming complexity and uncertainty, is to cultivate 'creative intelligence', which is a synthesis of intellectual, intuitive, and emotional intelligence. And this is a consequence of a deeper level of consciousness – and expanded awareness of one's real Self (see Fig. 1.8). We shall deal with this aspect in the Parts Two and Three.

'The problems we have today cannot be solved at the level of thinking we were at when we created them.'

The point is, however, that to keep abreast with the latest and relevant ideas, one has to think differently – keep one's mind open, free from any biases or prejudices. To recall Einstein's most frequently quoted statement, 'The problems we have today cannot be solved at the level of thinking we were at when we created them.' Subsequently, perhaps with some sadness, he says 'With the

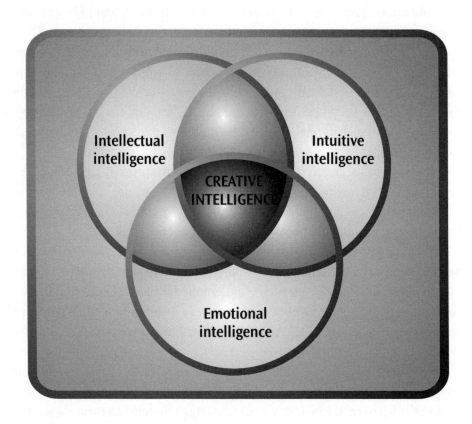

Fig. 1.8 Creative intelligence.

advent of quantum mechanics, everything has changed save our level of thinking and thus we drift toward unparalleled disaster'.

The point is that to make a difference in our lives, i.e. in our relationships, we have to think differently and feel differently; only then we can function differently, relate differently. The most powerful thing today is the new idea whose time has come; at the same time the most helpful thing is to drop the idea whose end has come!

Remember, our minds are like parachutes – they work best when they are open!

Our minds are like parachutes – they work best when they are open!

PUBLIC LEVEL

Our relationships at all the above described levels are within the context of our positioning ourselves as a member of society. But what is society? At one level it is a concrete and specific entity, namely the local society in which we live and work. In a broader sense it is the national, or the global or in the most general sense the whole of humanity. The profile of our contemporary society unfortunately indicates that even after several centuries of economic and technological advances, there are continuing conflicts – social, political, religious, and ethnic at all levels of society – indicating that we have not been able to relate appropriately to each other in our public life, or to the society as a whole. We have already discussed these 'paradoxes of success' earlier, in the Introduction. Key issues: *civic and social responsibility*.

Relationship with inner self

Ralph Waldo Emerson once wrote that history is 'the length and shadow of a man'. By this he could have implied that an individual could dominate his or her times to the extent of shaping them entirely. But there is another possible meaning for this felicitous phrase. Our personal history as people who lead public lives – lives in history – is also shaped by our 'shadow' selves, the part of us no one can ever fully know, not even ourselves. Our goal as unique individuals living in society is to be true to ourselves while at the same time being true to the society in which we live.

Each one of us has a public life – the part of our lives we live for our community, our nation, our world. It is with this life in mind that we rise above our selfish aims and do things for larger purposes. If we were to sum up our lives in epitaphs, it would be this broad public dimension that we might offer as our ultimate identity.

Ideally, our public persona and our private person – our inner self – should be congruent – there should not be any conflict between our personal agenda and public activities. This has been the case with several personalities throughout history. This would be possible if we relate to our inner self and experience our self-identity beyond our self-centred ego-self – our life then could be authentically transparent as our public activities become our personal agenda: our actions would be guided by what is in public interest.

Relationship with other people

Without relationship with other people, there would be no 'public' dimension to our lives. The very term 'public', traceable to the old Latin word *publicus*, means people. Yet whereas all our 'public' relationships involve people, not all of our relationships with people are public. In fact, there is a very distinct dynamic in our 'public' relationships with people.

Therefore when we are talking about relationships with people at the public level, we are referring to our relationships with people, our basic attitudes towards people, in general, in our public activities. Mainly, the issue here would be whether one inherently does or does not like to interact with people and whether one has the necessary skills for it. If one is oriented towards, and interested in, involvement with public activities, then having the relevant attitudes and skills becomes crucial to achieving success and satisfaction while relating to people in public. This would be especially true for those interested in political activities.

Relationships with things

Just as in our personal and professional lives we have relationships with things, so too in our public life we have meaningful relationships. The most important and lasting relationships at this level are those with historic national monuments with international impact. We have an everlasting relationship with the Taj Mahal, the Pyramids, the Arc De Triomphe, Big Ben, the Statue of Liberty, Fujiyama, the Wall of China and so on.

Physical things, man-made or natural, have a unique power to create or absorb the passions and prejudices of a people in the public aspect of their existence. Why else would their be monuments built on graves of significant persons? Why else would there be statues in public parks and places? Why else would nations have flags? These objects generate an ongoing relationship and transmit our values as nothing else can. People come and go; they change, they age, they thrill, they disappoint. So does our self and the ideas and events of our lives. But things continue to embody and reflect our continuing relationships at a public level.

Relationship with events

The intensity or otherwise of our relationship with public events, could be measured from the eagerness with which we await the daily newspaper! Our whole life is a series of events – private and public. With regard to public events, our relationship with them will obviously depend on the level of our interest and involvement in the specific area of the concerned event, whether it is political, social, academic, artistic, religious, professional, sporting, etc.

The main issue in this regard is the exponential rise in the amount of activity and events of all sorts around us everyday and despite our real interest in several of these events, our finite resources in terms of time, talent, energy and finance would severely affect how we relate and involve ourselves in such events. In this regard, our ability to prioritize, according to our needs, values and competencies, and consciously to balance our personal, professional, and public lives, would play a very crucial and decisive role in determining the depth and direction of our relationship with events in our public lives.

Relationship with ideas
In our public lives, we also have a relationship with ideas. These are manifested in the way we function with, or relate to, the various features that determine the profile of our society. A few examples follow.

Firstly, our idea about 'work'. Originally, we pursued work as a means of sustenance. Now, we work to earn an income beyond mere sustenance. It is with greater frequency that we now keep hearing, especially from younger people, about pursuit of work as a source of fulfillment – work to satisfy not only an economic need but also a psychological imperative.

Similarly, our idea about our environment and therefore our relationship with the environment has also been changing. Originally we were subservient to nature. Then we started dominating it. Now, because we are threatened about the excessive pollution and its dangerous consequences, there is an increasing pressure on us to provide more intelligent and enlightened stewardship in relating to our environment. It is a similar case with our natural resources. We used them, now we are still exploiting them despite rising voices for sustainable development.

As another example, it is because our changing ideas about the role of women in society, that the treatment of women has changed significantly from the earlier role as one with the primary responsibility for the home and family to considering them as 'full partners in progress'.

Therefore, it is how we relate to *ideas* in our public lives that determines the profile of our society.

***

So far, we have taken an overview of the various levels, dimensions, and types of relationships in our lives and considered, rather briefly, some of the issues we face with respect to these relationships. In doing so, the objective was to provide a sketch, by no means exhaustive, just to provide a glimpse of the deep and complex world of relationships. With this backdrop, we can now explore more elaborately the dynamics of the multilevel and multidimensional relationships that constitute our lives.

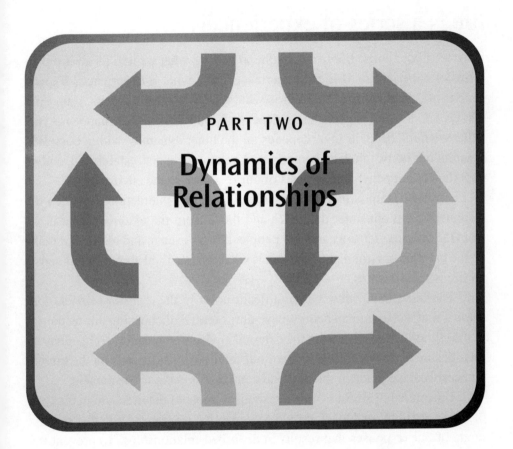

PART TWO

Dynamics of Relationships

In simple terms, life is a series of experiences.

If we recall our entire life from childhood to now, what we will recall is only a series of experiences. If life is experience, then, what is experience? Experience is not what happens to us. It is what we *do* to what happens to us. And what we *do* to what happens to us, depends upon what we *think* happens to us. What we *think* happens to us depends on the inner dynamics within ourselves – within our body, mind, and emotions. A relationship gets established, and an experience 'happens', on the basis of our response to the environment.

All life is relationships.

A relationship is therefore a series of ongoing interactions between the responses from our inner dynamics and those from the external dynamics – from the various elements, namely people, things, events, and ideas, that make up the external environment. And that is what our life is all about! In this sense, all life is relationships.

The most interesting and significant point in the *dynamics of relationships* is that we, as human beings, have the potential of choosing our responses to the stimuli we receive from the external environment, and thereby alter our relationships, our life. The quality of our relationships depends on the kind of choices we have made in the past and continue to make in the present.

Unfortunately, most people's responses, most of the time, are in the form of 'fight or flight' or 'attack or avoid' – reactive responses. It is this reactive mode of our responses that results in disturbed relationships. To prevent this and to enable us to manage our relationships in a desirable and durable manner, we need to understand, more deeply, the 'inner dynamics' within our selves as well as the 'outer dynamics'. This will enable us to acquire the ability to choose our responses – to become truly proactive and creative.

THE INNER DYNAMICS – 'SELF-RELATIONSHIP'

Who am I? Who are you? In Part One, we discussed this aspect quite elaborately, and discovered that we are not just our body, our mind, or our emotions. We clarified that these were mainly the functional aspects of the self. In fact, the persistent conflicts that we experience in our life and work are largely due to the mistaken identity that we give to ourselves by assuming that we are what is ours – our ego-self.

So who are we really? While we have already gone over this issue, it would be useful to repeat this approach for understanding more clearly the dynamics of our relationship with our Self; because it is on this understanding that the dynamics of all our other relationships depends.

The dynamics, the interactions, the 'relationships' among our body, mind, and emotions, are the ego-self or 'me'. Each of these three is a unique and integral part of me but they are not my real self. *The real Self is the inner 'I', the awareness, the consciousness, a kind of constant 'observer' or 'witness' throughout my life – the centered Self, the proactive, the creative Self,* as explained in Part One. All change, all positive growth can take place at that important twilight zone between the 'me' – the functional areas of my Self of which I am aware –and the 'I' –the centered Self that is aware.

The persistent conflicts that we experience in our life and work are largely due to the mistaken identity that we give to ourselves by assuming that we are what is ours

This 'I', the inner self, is the proactive Self, the arena of discretion, the level from which we can choose our responses. This is also the level of awareness, which is the source of real creativity – creative intelligence, which is the synthesis of intellectual intelligence, intuitive intelligence, and emotional intelligence.

Remaining in touch with this level of the Self – the observing self, the managing self, or the centered self – which is 'aware', proactive and creative, and remaining detached from our ego-self, and functioning accordingly in our various outer relationships with people, things, ideas, and events, gives us the freedom and the power to be 'in charge', 'in control', of our actions, our behavior, our experience of life.

This is our real empowerment; this enables us to perceive any situation with equanimity and act creatively, transforming our behavior from inner ego-related, self-centered reactive inner compulsions to proactive inner control. Functioning from ego-identity generates reactivity, the fight or flight, attack or avoid response, losing the power to act intelligently. This vitiates our relationships all around and corrodes our living potential.

THE OUTER DYNAMICS: THE COMPLEXITY OF RELATIONSHIPS

The process of understanding, experiencing and functioning from this deeper level of the Self enables us to find an appropriate balancing in our various 'outer' relationships – which are not only complex but often conflicting. If we do not operate from this centered self, then we find it extremely difficult to deal with these relationships effectively – or to manage and sustain them in a healthy and harmonious way.

The challenge, first of all, is clearly in our relationships with *people*. Even creating and sustaining a relationship with one individual is difficult. There are always ups and downs and conflicts of various kinds. Superimpose on that our relationships with other people, such as our extended family. This generates complexity, which frequently leads to conflicting interests and disturbed relationships.

Imagine, now, the amount of complexity that is multiplied when we think about not only the relationships at home but at work and elsewhere. Here, too, there are all these continuous ups and downs and conflicts which demand and drain a lot of energy.

Then superimpose on all that our relationships with *things* that we want to have, use and enjoy. There again there is a conflict among our relationships within various things, between 'needs' and 'niceties', just as there is a kind of built-in conflict in our relationships with different people. There are always juxtaposed and conflicting relationships among things we desire. To maintain a balanced relationship among the often conflicting claims of various things we need to have a clear and proactive sense of our priorities.

Again on top of all this, we have to consider our relationships with *events* and *ideas*.

We have therefore to recognize that the world of relationships is far more complex than what we may have imagined. This complexity generates a lot of stress, turmoil, and dissatisfaction – and even sometimes illnesses. Eventually this can, and unfortunately does, lead many otherwise desirable relationships to break down prematurely and corrode the richness of our lives.

It should therefore be realized that managing relationships efficiently and effectively requires specialized expertise and committed efforts. Ordinary intelligence, or common sense, by itself is not adequate for dealing with the subtle and peculiar dynamics of relationships. In fact, one has to function by remaining in touch with, involved with our proactive self – the missing link – detached from the reactive ego-self, but functioning *through* the ego self, with which all the relationships are 'related'. Functioning with such 'detached involvement' can enable us to manage all our relationships in a manner that ensures a rich, harmonious, intelligent and meaningful life.

Why? And how? Once again, let it be emphasized that the ego level, the normal, the so-called intellectual or rational level at which we generally function, is quite simply, by its very nature, self-centered or selfish, which often results in multiple conflicts. This is the central reason for fractured and disrupted relationships. To achieve harmony in our relationships and peace in our minds, we need to detach ourselves from the 'me' or ego-self. If we have a detached and deeper perception, which grows with our experience of our real identity as the centered Self, then we can perceive all these fractured relationships and conflicts around us dissolving into complementarities.

To achieve harmony in our relationships and peace in our minds, we need to detach ourselves from the 'me' or ego-self.

Let us take a hypothetical example indicating a usual reaction to a situation.

At random, we will select a personal relationship in the present, a relationship with people: two friends, A and B; and one from the past: A and his parents. We will also choose an aspect of that relationship, positive chemistry turning neutral or negative, and a level affecting that relationship – the managerial level: A and B are also co-workers. Then at random, we will pick a relationship with a thing (alcohol) an event (my loss of a job), and an idea (capitalism) – and add in an issue with the inner self (search for self esteem). So the story of relationships here might go something like this:

> *A and B have always gotten along very well. They work at the same company. Recently, A and B came to know that A would be losing his job. It seemed to A that B was becoming a bit more distant, as if he was pulling away from him. A thought that B was doing so because he might be feeling uncomfortable that he would be continuing with his job even after A's job was terminated. Both of them used to go for a beer after work, but now A found himself going out alone. As he was having his drink, he began to reflect on the loss of his job, how difficult it would be to get another one, how the whole economic system is defective which creates such frustration and insecurity, there should be some protection for workers … but then he had never felt protected – not even in his childhood as he was growing up; his folks always said that he would be a failure … and it looks as if he has become one …*

This is a fairly typical situation and pattern. In fact, things frequently do get even worse and more complicated, if we consider all the other levels, dimensions, types and profiles of all the relevant relationships.

We are called to break out of the cocoon of the ego-involved relationships, to be free – and deepen our relationships with detached involvement.

If relationships manifested themselves as 'threads', at any given moment in time we would probably see literally hundreds of strands around us – we could barely move! And the more negative emotions we have connected with these relationships, the more paralyzed we become.

So here we are, surrounded by threads everywhere. How do we move forward or move at all? The solution lies within us. Whether to consider the threads as a cobweb or links or opportunities for a rich and vibrant life, rests with us – our perceptions and positioning. If we visualize the threads of our relationships as a cocoon, and our inner self as a potential butterfly, the message is clear. We are called to break out of the cocoon of the ego-involved relationships, to be free – and deepen our relationships with detached involvement.

In other words, the precondition for managing relationships in a healthy and sustainable way is managing the relationship with our own true self – the I, not just the me. If we can answer the question 'Who am I?' in an authentic way and with a higher level of perception, we can avoid living a life with a mistaken identity, at the limited ego-centered self, which frequently results in internal conflicts, splintered or broken external relationships and suboptimal living.

The precondition for managing relationships in a healthy and sustainable way is managing the relationship with our own true self.

THE TRAJECTORY OF LIFE DYNAMICS – EVOLUTION OF SELF-IDENTITY

Now, it is important to clarify here that ego, by itself, is not bad. Indeed, the ego is absolutely essential, not only for our psychic survival, but also for interacting and relating with the outer dynamics of people, things, events and ideas.

It is also the starting point in the trajectory of our life, which passes through three phases:

◆ In the first phase, we develop the ego-self, 'shoring up' the ego. This may go on into one's teens, 20s or sometimes even 30s (it varies for individuals) and it is vital not only for our self-identity and for our psychic survival, but also for our self-development.

◆ The second phase is ego maturity, 'sorting out' the ego. In this phase, we come to understand what is ego and who we really are and are not.

◆ Beyond ego maturity is the third level, 'soaring above' the ego: ego transcendence – the 'butterfly' stage, as mentioned earlier. We detach from the ego, and are no longer the ego. Instead we use the ego – we function through it. This is the level at which we should be functioning as conscious and intelligent adults.

The trajectory of life, then, is ego development, ego maturity and ego transcendence: shoring up, sorting out and soaring above the ego. Once we have soared above the ego and developed that identity or that real relationship with our true Self, then we can begin to perceive all the multiple and multilevel relationships with people, things, events, and ideas, in a more proactive, professional and balanced way. We can then optimize and enrich our relationships – plugging

The trajectory of life is shoring up, sorting out, and soaring above the ego.

the 'missing link' and enhancing the meaning and purpose of our life: *making a life while making a living*.

So what we really need is a synthesis, an appropriate link, between our self-centered ego level *selfish* needs and our *selfless* consciousness as a transcendent being, and function with 'Selfness'. We don't have to fulfill Benjamin Disraeli's wry observation that 'Youth is a blunder, manhood a struggle, old age a regret'. By cultivating a 'conscious' and resilient relationship between our inner dynamics and the outer dynamics, our youth can be a shoring up, our early adulthood a sorting, and older adulthood a soaring!

Our youth can be a shoring up, our early adulthood a sorting, and older adulthood a soaring!

Having considered the issues of our inner dynamics, basically our relationship with our Self and the ego-self, and also the 'internal reference point' of Selfness while dealing with the outer dynamics, now let us discuss how with such a positioning, we could relate with some of the critical issues of relationships.

GAPS: EXPECTATIONS VERSUS ACHIEVEMENT, INTENTION VERSUS ACTION

Our identification or overattachment with the ego-self leads to the generation of 'gaps': on the one hand, a gap between our expectations from the environment, the external dynamics, and the fulfillment of the same or our perceived achievement; and on the other hand, a gap between our intention to act or function in a certain way and our actual behavior. Both of these gaps cause internal frustration and possibly fracture in our external relationships.

Satisfaction is the function between expectation and achievement.

Satisfaction is the function between expectation and achievement, with reference to one's own action or performance as well as those of others. If they coincide there is satisfaction, but, unfortunately, quite often that is not the case. There is usually, for most people, a gap between what they expect and what they perceive as their achievement. In any relationship, there is some frustration and some satisfaction. Our usual desire and effort is to avoid or reduce frustration and increase satisfaction. How can we do that? The conceptual framework for this is actually quite simple and clear, though the dynamics may on surface appear to be complex.

Take an example of a relationship between A and B (see Fig. 2.1). Satisfaction for A results when the perceived achievement of A, of the behavior from B, is equal to or exceeds A's expectation from B. However, what quite often happens is described in the illustration, indicating the 'gaps' both A and B experience.

A has a certain expectation (area 1) from B, and his/her perception of B's action (area 2) falls short of his/her expectations (area 1), which causes frustration in A. And this affects A's behavior with B.

B, in turn, has the real intention (area 4) of more than fulfilling what s/he perceives as A's expectations (area 1). B's actual behavior or performance (area 3), even if it may fall short of B's own intentions (and this does usually happen), it may still be higher than B's perception of and A's actual expectations (area 1). Therefore, B assumes that A will be satisfied, and expects a certain acknowledgment, or at least an appropriate response, from A indicating his/her satisfaction. But, as we observed earlier, A is actually disappointed or frustrated with B's behavior, because his/her perception of B's behavior has fallen short of his/her expectations from B and therefore acts accordingly, creating

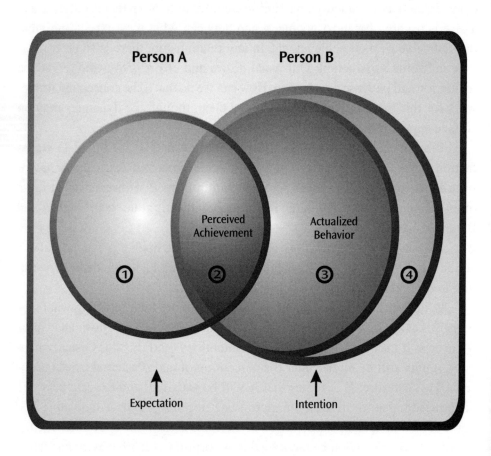

Fig. 2.1   Intention–action–perception–reaction.

frustration in B! There will also be another layer of frustration in B as his/her actual action falls short of his/her intentions. This obviously results in a negative tension in the relationship between A and B.

To get beyond this vicious spiral, which results in negative relationships, we should be:

1   more balanced/realistic in pegging one's expectations from others

2   focused more on others' intentions that just their actions

3   less reactive, less biased or prejudiced in one's perceptions and judgments.

One can achieve the above attitudes and approaches by remaining centered in the consciousness of detached involvement, as has been described and emphasized earlier and is further explained below.

As satisfaction is the difference between our expectations and our achievements, it is obvious that to increase our satisfaction, we must either increase our perceived achievements or decrease our expectations. In order to do either of these things, we must progressively diminish our identification with our ego-self, which generally tends to belittle our achievements (due to a common tendency of self-downing or over modesty – though for some it can be the opposite), even as it increases our expectations.

We should first keep in mind the difference between the intentions to achieve and the expectation of results while making the efforts to achieve.

We have to understand the subtlety of this issue very carefully. We should first keep in mind the difference between the *intentions to achieve* and the *expectation of results* while making the *efforts to achieve* ... Our intentions for achievements should always remain high. Otherwise, there will be no progress or development, but only stagnation and decay. What is indicated and advocated here is that while our intentions to achieve the fulfillment of our expectations (and our efforts towards that) may and should remain high, our expectations of results, *while we are making the efforts to achieve* the results, should neither be excessively high nor cynically low.

It is very interesting to know why it should be so. One thing that is often overlooked is that in our human psyche, whenever there is an expectation, there is always a concomitant anxiety about not fulfilling the expectation. And such anxiety contaminates our efforts, our performance, the process necessary to achieve the results, to fulfill our expectations.

With detached involvement, several things would happen:

◆ First, we would be able to pitch our intentions for achievement and expectations in a proactive and balanced way, keeping in mind on the one hand the need for a strong driving force within for continued progress, and on the other hand the practical realism to prevent excessive wishful thinking.

◆ Second, we would also perceive our achievements in a proactive and balanced manner, without reactive bias and prejudice.

◆ Third – and this is crucial – even if there is a significant gap, either way, between our expectation and perceived achievement, our identity with our inner self, the true self, will enable us to function with detached involvement and prevent either undue elation or reactive depression.

◆ Finally, with such a balanced approach we would be able to manage the dynamics of our relationships at an appropriate level, increasing our satisfaction and decreasing frustration.

An illustration of the kind of dynamics that could emerge with such an approach is described in Fig. 2.2.

GRAVITIES

We have already briefly considered this concept in Part One, while discussing the issue of relationship with events. We will once again take it up here.

To repeat what has already been emphasized, there is gravity here on earth. We are also aware that this gravity severely limits our freedom of movement and regulates our lives in a variety of ways. Ordinarily, if anything or anyone limits or curbs our freedom, we immediately resist and protest. However, no one seems to be protesting against gravity! Why not? The reason is that everyone has accepted that gravity is a totally unchangeable fact of life. It is one of the great gifts of nature to the human psyche that, if we realize that something is totally unchangeable, then we tend to relate to it with not only

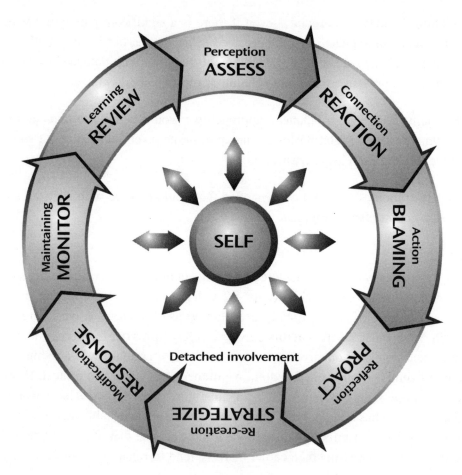

Fig. 2.2   Dynamics of detached involvement.

passive acceptance, but also quite often with an attitude of actively learning to adjust to it – and without any negative feeling.

Now, let us consider whether there are any things or situations in our lives with the same character as that of gravity: totally unchangeable, either for ever or within a specified period of time. If we find that, indeed, there are such unchangeable 'gravities' in our lives, then we should clearly identify them and learn to relate to them accordingly.

If we look at our different levels of living, personal, professional, and public, we will discover several such gravities at each of these levels. (See Fig. 1.4).

Personal level

For example, to repeat what has already been mentioned earlier, there are several physical aspects or features of our body that cannot be changed during our entire life and some, for example weight, which are not changeable for a specified period – of say, one year, three months, one week or even one day. Moreover, there are similar changeable or non-changeable 'gravities' in other dimensions of our mental and emotional self, either for our entire lifetime or over a specific period of time.

Thinking about our lifetime, during the next ten years or a given time span, what is unchangeable? Several things may come to our mind such as death, aging, our past, chronic ailments, etc. In each of these cases, we may have negative feelings. This is almost a universal phenomenon – almost everyone feels negative about such situations – and it seems quite natural to relate negatively to them. In fact, however, this would not be very intelligent, because even if we may have negative feelings about them and even if we ceaselessly try to change any of them, as they are non-changeable like gravity, nothing is really going to change! This is only going to result in frustration, and an under-current of negative feelings.

Again, here also, let us be careful in understanding this notion. The idea is not to say that one should do nothing about the phenomenon of death, aging, or terminal illness. Of course, for example, one should definitely try to do all that is possible and necessary to make death as postponable and painless as possible. But the point is that while making all such efforts, one should not be tormented by negative feelings. One should try to face the events with 'acceptance', otherwise the experience of negative feelings would, in fact, worsen the situation and may even intensify the problem and accelerate the culmination of the event.

Professional level

Similarly, at the professional level, at the workplace there may be several people, things, events, or even ideas in terms of the organization's culture and strategies, that one may not like or may not be able to relate to in a comfortable way. But, after considering any of these in an objective, sincere and honest way, if one concludes that for the time being, or within a specified period of time, no matter what one does those elements are not going to change, that they are 'gravities', then one has to relate to them as such and learn to live with them with minimum negative feeling (for the specific period). By relating to such gravities in this manner, one will prevent a constant negative feeling about them, which drains ones energy, and becomes counterproductive. One important and positive consequence of this would be that of enabling one to focus one's energy and attention positively towards elements that could be changed.

Public level

The same applies to 'gravities' at the public level. For example, if one has chosen to live in a particular area or community, and there are some features about them that are not agreeable but are 'gravities', then one has to learn to accept and adjust to them. At the same time, if any of these 'gravities' appear to be changeable over a period of time through sustained effort, then, while accepting to live with them for the present, and without any negative reactivity about them, one should continue to make the efforts proactively to alter them.

We frequently become agitated over things or situations that are unchangeable within a particular time frame. We fritter away our emotions, energies and resources and disturb some of our important relationships, trying to change such gravities. Moreover, there are several other things and situations that we can influence and change, but if our attention and energies are preoccupied or engaged in such a dysfunctional way (trying to change the unchangeable), the effectiveness of our efforts in other areas, and our relationships, will be seriously and adversely affected.

Therefore, to be intelligent in our relationships with the various internal and external elements in our lives, we need to identify explicitly at various levels – personal, professional and public – what are the gravities and what are not. This will enable us to position our relationships with them more effectively and enable us to make a more judicious allocation of our limited energies and resources. By setting proper priorities we can, over a period, bring about maximum amount of possible change and minimize the gravities around us.

It should once again be emphasized that this approach does not imply a passive or fatalistic acceptance of everything. Quite the contrary. It implies that if we want to be appropriate in our relationships and be more effective in our 'change' strategies, we have to apply our limited resources in a proactive and prioritized manner, rather than dissipating them on a more reactive emotional or prejudiced basis.

It should also be noted that there may be specific situations or things where we cannot be absolutely sure whether they are really gravities or 'changeabilities' – and therefore treat them with a kind of tentativeness. That is why the line in the figure indicating gravities (Fig. 1.4 seen earlier) is dotted, not solid.

The critical issue is that we have to use this approach honestly and objectively; otherwise, of course, there would be a danger of becoming complacent or passive, or even irresponsible, by treating most things as unchangeable. Therefore, before we treat any situation as a gravity, we must make doubly sure, honestly and objectively, that it is really so. We must remember that this approach is only a tool or an instrument. Every tool or instrument can be used as well as abused. A knife in the hands of a skilled surgeon can save a life, but the same knife in the hands of an irresponsible citizen can take a life!

Every tool or instrument can be used as well as abused.

LIVING WITH THE REALITIES OF GAPS AND GRAVITIES

How can we put into practice our understanding of the many types and levels of relationships? How can we respond to the gaps we experience in relation to other people, and to the gravities in our relationship with things and events?

We begin by being intelligently aware of them, and identifying and accepting them as such. Thinking about all our people relationships, we can come to understand the expectations we have of others and the expectations others have of us. We have to accept the fact that these may seldom match perfectly. And thinking about all the events in our lives, we can come to understand that some aspects, whether we like it or not, are like gravity: aging, illness, death, our past, etc.

Keeping in mind the possibility of repositioning our self-identity from the reactive ego-self to the inner proactive Self, and relating to everything from that position, as explained earlier, we can accept and learn to live with the 'gaps' and 'gravities', without any, or with a minimum, negative feeling. This would then enable us to move forward with our lives more freely and energetically, more positively and proactively, and should really make a desirable difference in our relationships.

Revisiting our earlier example of the two friends, A and B, with such an understanding, A could begin to think differently:

'My friend must have some other reason for pulling away from me. Maybe he thinks that I might feel uncomfortable or embarrassed talking to him about my losing my job or maybe he thinks I might be feeling

jealous of him ... Perhaps I should not be so reactive to this and maybe I should take a proactive initiative and clarify my feelings, and if possible revive my relationship with him.

It is disappointing that I have lost my job, but it is really not a disaster or the end of the road. This should not lead to depression. I still have my dignity – no one can take that away from me. I can get another job. I must find out what is it that led to my losing my job this time, so that I can prevent it from happening again ...

I must accept this event as Gravity for the present. I do value B's friendship and it is certainly worth much more than the alcohol that has been keeping me company recently ...

No matter under what system things are being run today or what people may think or say about me, I still have enough space really to live my life successfully. In my next job, I should try to improve my performance.

It is not fair to blame my parents, or any one else, for my present situation. After all, I did have the opportunities. I could have prevented this situation if I had been less tardy and more alert and responsible. Maybe, this jolt was necessary to wake me up and shake out my passive and 'blaming others' tendency ...

Actually, as a responsible person and citizen, I can and should relate to everything around me more sensibly, and try my best to make a positive difference.'

THE 'DABDA' EFFECT (Denial-Anger-Bargaining-Depression-Acceptance)

Let us now consider how we relate to some very negative situations. Generally, our initial psychological response to unfavorable news begins with **D**enial, **A**nger, and **B**argaining. The immediate mental dialogue, quite commonly, is something along these lines: 'No, this can't be true…': when it is realized that the news is true, the next response is usually anger. 'How could this happen to me, why me, why now …?' Sometimes, in a complaining mode, one may develop an 'other blaming' attitude, and perhaps get angry even with 'God' – 'how unjust and unfair He is …!' After going through such initial emotional reactions, then one begins to rationalize 'After all, this is not all that bad …' And one may recall the famous four magic words: ' It could be worse'. Only after going through a lot of such suffering does one settle down to a feeling of sadness or **D**epression, and ultimately, with the passage of time, one **A**ccepts the situation as a 'gravity' – and relates to it as an unchangeable reality.

Instead of going through the above described, commonly experienced sequence of suffering (and this could be quite prolonged, and perhaps for some even permanent), one should relate to such situations more intelligently and proactively by analyzing them, at the initial stage only, into gravity or changeable, and relating to them accordingly. By cultivating such an approach and attitude we can prevent a lot of suffering as well as protect some relationships.

There should be a basic understanding that, generally speaking, we cannot control external phenomena in any significant way, but we can control our attitudes towards them. If we cannot change the 'winds' we can at least reposition

If we cannot change the 'winds' we can at least reposition the 'sails'!

the 'sails'! And if the road ahead is rocky and we are unable to cover it with leather (or no one rolls out a red carpet!), it would be wise to wear shoes!

The essence of managing the dynamics of relationships, is cultivating the qualities and competencies required for bringing about an ongoing balance within one's inner dynamics of body, mind and emotions, and thereby enhancing harmony with the external dynamics of relationships with people, things, events and ideas – integrating the inner with the outer.

In Part three, we will see how to deepen our relationships through the one central concept that ties all of this together: detached involvement.

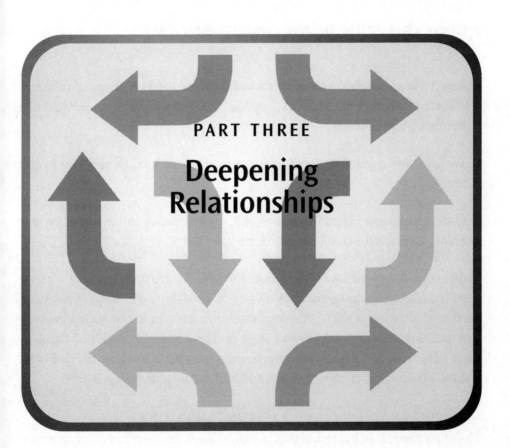

PART THREE

Deepening
Relationships

In journeying through this book, we have made the following observations:

◆ Reality is a complex web of relationships. Our life is a series of relationships. Life is experience, and experience is the consequence of how we relate to other 'relationships'.

◆ We have many relationships – with our selves, people, things, events and ideas.

◆ Our success and happiness in life and work depends in large part on our ability to manage relationships effectively.

In this concluding part, we will explore the knowledge, skills and attitudes we need for effective management of all our relationships. We will consider the need to change our level of thinking, minimize the barriers to such a change, and reaching a 'condition' beyond these barriers, namely, 'detached involvement'. This is a precondition for acquiring the requisite know-how, the feel-how, and the do-how, for creating meaningful and sustainable relationships.

ACQUIRING KNOWLEDGE VERSUS APPLYING KNOWLEDGE
The many threads of our relationships can be a prison in our lives – or a cocoon for growth. Which will it be? We can choose growth if we understand how to

put into practice some of the concepts we have already explored so far.

In the flooding river of management concepts, and in the sea of self-help and how-to books and groups, there are many useful ideas. However, despite the continuing torrent of new ideas, most of us find it difficult to put them into practice. And so the gap between our knowledge and our performance or behavior, between what we want to do and what we are able to do, continues to grow.

The gap between what we want to do and what we are able to do continues to grow.

To close this gap, we must begin by addressing the basic question, namely, 'Why is there such a gap between knowledge and performance?' or 'What is the real barrier?' The answer is that there is a discrepancy in our relationships, a gap between how we generally relate to our relationships and how we should actually be relating to them.

This is a known and acknowledged fact. But despite this knowledge, we are still not able to relate or behave differently. Basically, what we need to realize is the fact that *acquiring* knowledge is not the same thing as *applying* knowledge. Even when we read a book or attend a seminar, we may experience some 'Eureka' moments or 'aha' clicks, experience a real 'stretch' in our thinking, and we walk away satisfied and excited about our 'learnings' and with a sincere desire and commitment to implement the new ideas immediately.

Acquiring knowledge is not the same thing as applying knowledge.

However, while the 'halo' effect of the book or the seminar may continue for a week or two, sooner than we may realize, quite often we find ourselves almost back to square one! For example, it would be pertinent to ask, whether leadership around us has really improved in the last few years, despite an exponential rise in different models of leadership during the last decade. Do we really have better leaders today in various fields and levels of our society:

political, social, economic or academic or even religious? Unfortunately, it does not seem so.

But, this should not imply that knowledge is not useful. In fact, it is essential. We must continue to acquire relevant knowledge. But the point is that knowledge *by itself* is not enough. To convert knowledge into performance or behavior, we do not need just more knowledge – we need more courage. And this can be acquired and experienced only at another 'level' of thinking and feeling, possible only at another level of consciousness or self-identity.

It would be pertinent once again to recall the statements of Einstein that we referred to earlier, which emphasized the need to develop another level of thinking if we want to cope with the issues, the problems and paradoxes we are facing today.

David Bohm describes this more succinctly. He says 'Trying to reassemble the fragments of a broken mirror to see a true reflection, is a futile task.'

The underlying issue in all this, is about changing our thinking from a reactive level to a proactive and creative level, to enable us to convert our knowledge into performance and behavior, leading to appropriate relationships. Most of us are quite aware of this. But, then, despite such awareness, why do we not change?

BARRIERS TO CHANGE

The first barrier is our relationship with change, the inner conflict we experience whenever we face change. This is a strange paradox in human behavior. On the one hand, as a living system, we have an instinctive urge for growth and

To convert knowledge into performance or behavior, we do not need just more knowledge – we need more courage.

'Trying to reassemble the fragments of a broken mirror to see a true reflection, is a futile task.'

change. We are self-organizing, self-renewing, interacting systems (auto-poesis and auto-catalysis). At the same time, we have a tendency also to resist change at an instinctive level. We have a basic need for security and survival, continuity and consistency, and generally any stimulus for change generates discomfort and insecurity. We have, at a subconscious level, a craving to remain in our stable, non-changing 'comfort zone'!

Even from the psycho-neurological standpoint, our thinking process is a pattern-forming and pattern-reinforcing system. We form an opinion, viewpoint or belief, and then perceive and receive only information that reinforces (or can be reshaped to reinforce) this existing pattern or belief. Whatever is in conflict with our existing mental models or mindsets, we have a tendency to resist and often reject. In this sense, we have a natural barrier that constrains our ability to change and even receive, let alone apply, any new knowledge that does not 'fit' in our existing mental frameworks.

In this context, it would be interesting to take the metaphor of a 'seed' to understand this paradox. A seed has tremendous potential for change and growth. At the same time, inside, it can give a great feeling of comfort. The choice then would be to remain as a seed, feeling secure in the comfort zone, or to have the courage to fertilize and nurture the seed appropriately so that it can break open and blossom into a full grown plant with fruits or flowers!

The *second barrier* is our relationship with our self, our ego-identity – our identification with our ego dynamics of body, mind, and emotion. If, for example, we relate and identify ourselves with our mind, our existing thinking and beliefs, it becomes very difficult to change them, as that would imply destroying our very identity! This creates the barrier to change, because, if we want to bring about change, the essential precondition for change is to change our beliefs, our current level of thinking, as discussed above.

We need to cultivate the consciousness and courage to move beyond our ego.

Therefore, we need to cultivate the consciousness and courage to move beyond our ego-identity to convert our knowledge into the desired behavior. We can then stop identifying ourselves with our mind, our thinking, or belief systems, and begin to detach and liberate ourselves from them. This freedom in turn will enhance the proactive courage we need to keep our minds open to receiving new, even divergent knowledge, and change our level of thinking, feeling, and doing – making our relationships more meaningful and effective. What we need most today therefore is not more conventional knowledge, but more courage. And courage cannot just come to us by merely desiring it. *Courage is a consequence of a higher level of consciousness, a self-identity beyond our skin-encapsulated ego-identity.*

In order to remain stable in a changing world, we have to change.

With courage, our relationship with change will be more positive – we may begin to consider change not only as giving up or losing something, but as an 'ex-change' – getting, in return, something more relevant and desirable. It might, in a sense, make us feel more secure in a more intelligent way by realizing that in order to remain stable in a changing world, we have to change.

Then the question is, how does one acquire or achieve this 'higher' level of consciousness or altered self-identity?

MANAGING BY DETACHED INVOLVEMENT

The key to transcending these barriers of ego-identity and change -resistance is *detached involvement:* an expanded level of consciousness, of relationship, of self-identity, that can bridge the gap between knowledge and behavior, between what we like to do, what we have to do, and what we are able to do.

Detached involvement enables us to develop and deepen a different level and quality of relationship with our self and our inner dynamics. Paradoxical as it may seem, detachment leads to an expanded relationship with our Self, and involvement from such an expanded Self-relationship leads to a deeper and more authentic relationship with our inner body–mind–emotion dynamics. With such an expanded as well as deeper relationship within our selves, we can begin to perceive and relate to our outer dynamics and relationships, with a more proactive and creative attitude.

Basically, therefore, proactive management of our relationships provides the missing link between making a life and making a living. It generates the courage we need to harmonize cognition and action; facilitates the attitudes we need to harmonize vision, values, and performance; and enhances the feeling we need to convert thinking into doing.

The transition from ego attachment to detached involvement begins to raise our awareness, experience, and identification with a higher level of consciousness or the Self. In so doing it positions us in a proactive posture, an arena of discretion, from where we can choose and implement our responses from a different level of thinking. How and why? Because, in such a state, we remain detached from our reactive, self-centered, thoughts and emotions which, if not managed effectively, can become the sources of our psycho-neurological barriers and inner compulsions. With detached involvement we move from a

Detached involvement enables us to develop and deepen a different level and quality of relationship with our self and our inner dynamics.

Proactive management of our relationships provides the missing link between making a life and making a living.

state of inner compulsions to inner control, and achieve the freedom and courage to relate to our inner and outer dynamics proactively and ensure meaningful and sustainable relationships.

Managing by detached involvement is not just a tool or a skill; it is a way of life.

So far, there has been frequent repetition of this notion, perhaps a bit overdone, but the objective is to enable grasping of its essence thoroughly and internalizing the same. Essentially, managing by detached involvement is not just a tool or a skill; it is a way of life, a way of relating to reality and deepening our overall relationships.

Let us explore this concept further to understand its implications more clearly.

TWO ANALOGIES

Two analogies may explain the condition of detached involvement in more practical terms.

Consider your relationship to the chair you are sitting in. As long as you remain on it or in it – in a sense, as long as you remain identified with it – can you observe the whole chair? Obviously not. What do you need to do in order to observe the chair more fully? Again the obvious response would be that you need to get out of the chair to be able to observe the chair. But before you can consider the possibility of getting out of the chair, you will first have to accept intellectually that *you are not the chair* – that you are only the owner, the user, the occupier or the manager of the chair. Once you accept this 'relationship', you can then be motivated and begin to make the effort and get out of the chair by detaching and distancing yourself a little from the chair, enough to enable you still to have a link with the chair with one of your hands remaining in touch with the chair. *Now,* you can observe the chair more fully, almost the whole of it.

In this process of observing the chair, which necessitated your getting out of the chair, something very interesting and significant is happening. When you are in the chair, not only can you not observe the chair fully, but while in this condition, you cannot also move the chair or manage it! In fact, the chair, in a sense, manages you! – Your entire physical posture is controlled or managed by the physical chair.

From this we can distill the first law of human relationships: *'you can never relate to or manage effectively, that with which you are identified or over attached. And, whatever you are attached to or identified with, manages you.'* Any object of addiction or overattachment, living or otherwise, will always dominate you, 'manage' you.

When you are out of the chair, you would still be in contact with the chair as your hand should remain in touch with the chair all the time. Now in this position, not only can you observe almost the whole chair, you can also lift the chair, lead the chair, move the chair in the direction you choose, at the pace and in the manner *you* choose. Paradoxical as it may sound, when you are out of the chair, detached from the chair, you are the master of the chair!

This gives us the second law of human relationships: *'You can relate to or manage far more effectively, that (any person, thing, event, or idea) from which you are somewhat detached, not overly involved, or with which you have detached involvement.'*

The eye can see other things but not itself; the finger can touch other objects but not itself.

The eye can see other things but not itself; the finger can touch other objects but not itself.

The second analogy is that of the steering wheel of a car. Consider the way you relate to the steering wheel, the way you hold it while driving. When you first sat in the car, behind the steering wheel, to learn how to drive the car, you must have held the wheel tightly. There were so many overwhelming variables to cope with while driving, that the only anchor you had was the steering wheel. And therefore, as a learner, you must have held on to the wheel tightly – an illusion of control! But once you have been driving for some time, how would you hold the wheel? Much more lightly, – not too tight, not too loose – to enable you to drive smoothly with mastery: a balanced loose–tight, 'detached–involved' relationship with the wheel. If you hold the wheel more tightly or more loosely, your driving will suffer!

It would be a good idea to keep these two analogies in mind, as we are frequently in a chair or in a car. This will constantly keep us reminded of the power of detached involvement: courageous and creative proactivity.

It should be emphasized, however, that detachment should never imply withdrawal, or escape, or even indifference; and involvement should never imply addiction or 'imprisonment' – it implies 'interestedness'. It is this subtle balance, apparently a paradoxical condition, but one which gives us the unique power to effectively manage our paradoxical and often conflicting relationships.

It is also in this state, that we get the power and courage to function with integrity and honesty as our thinking and motivations do not get contaminated by our ego-driven selfishness and fear. Moreover, in this level of consciousness, we also experience a kind of universal connectedness and interdependence, which generates an authentic and deep compassion in us for all our relationships. And finally, such consciousness implies a genuine, positive, and charismatic energy in us, which creates resonance in our relationships: the key success factor in all levels, dimensions, and roles in our lives.

THE ROLE OF VISION

Now to give a concrete form to the proactive and creative consciousness we can acquire and cultivate through detached involvement, let us consider the role of vision in our life and relationships. At a reactive level we tend to be problem-driven. But in our era of accelerating change, complexity, and uncertainty, we need to be *vision-driven*.

In our era of accelerating change, complexity and uncertainty, we need to be vision driven.

Vision is a visual articulation of the desired state of the future. Having the driving force of a vision will enable us to perceive opportunities in our relationships rather than problems or conflicts. An essential precondition for a meaningful, harmonious, and sustainable relationship is not only to have a positive personal vision about relationship, but it should be a shared vision – beyond the ego-related, self-centered agenda, which often leads to conflicts. This means that our vision, that perception which motivates our life, should be shared by all those involved in any particular relationship, and aligned with the interests of all the other relationships.

THE PRIMACY OF VISION

Having a vision will not prevent us from being realistic or practical. Quite to the contrary, a vision is in fact essential in our complex and conflict-ridden

We need to have our heads high up in the skies but never lost in clouds, with our feet always firmly on the ground but never stuck in the mud.

world. To be able to lead a sensible, coherent, and dynamic life in such a contemporary environment, the usual analytical, mechanistic, and reductionist thinking is too limited, simplistic and fragmented: we need to cultivate more imaginative, intuitive and integrative thinking that can be a source of authentic vision building – a base for harmonious and sustainable relationships.

In other words, we have to be 'visionary pragmatists' ... This may sound self-contradictory. But this is precisely the approach we need to cultivate. We should be able to stretch our imagination to the maximum but within the arena of practical realism. We need to have our heads high up in the skies, but never lost in clouds; our feet should always be firmly on the ground, but never stuck in mud. If our head is above the clouds, the sun is always shining up there, we would always be bathed in 'sunshine' – positive, creative, life-sustaining energy! Occasionally, there may be some clouds blanketing the sun or sometimes even thunderstorms. But all this is below the level of the sun!

Metaphorically, in our present context, the sun represents the consciousness of detached involvement concretized into a vision. The clouds within are our ego-level reactive thinking that 'clouds' our perceptions, weakens our actions, and disturbs our relationships.

If our consciousness remains beyond this ego level, beyond the 'clouds', in touch with the perennial 'sunshine' – our vision – as a constant internal reference point, we walk on the 'ground' of our life – our relationships – with courage and equanimity.

As human beings we have a unique gift of nature, in as much as our minds can and do function simultaneously at multiple levels. Take the simple example of driving a car. While driving, one level of our mind is focused on the driving function, while another level would be either engaged in a dialogue with someone else in the car, or involved in thinking about some other issues. Driving and doing something else, both these functions, are performed simultaneously. Similarly, one level of our mind or awareness can remain in touch with our expanded consciousness or our vision, and the other level could be engaged in our various relationships. This is detached involvement, enabling our functioning as a visionary pragmatist to bring about a dynamic balance in our multi-level and multi-dimensional relationships.

THE SECOND COPERNICAN REVOLUTION

In the introduction, a reference was made to the contemporary information revolution. What we need now is a consciousness revolution – which can be deemed as a second Copernican revolution. The first Copernican revolution generated more accurate awareness and understanding about outer space, in particular that the earth is not the center of the universe – it is only one of the planets in a solar system. The second Copernican revolution can generate greater insight and consciousness about our inner space – that our ego is not the 'center' of our self, is not our real self, but only a dynamics of our body–mind–emotion. This would enable us to establish our relationship, our identity, with our true Self, and re-position our lives in the context of appropriate reality.

The second Copernican revolution can generate greater insight and consciousness about our inner space.

This is the essence of detached involvement – being authentically proactive and creative in the 'real' world, without any reactive attitudes of 'attack' or 'avoidance', escapes or excuses. It enables us to acquire a proactive, charismatic and constructive 'response-ability', especially in human relationships.

Once again I would like to repeat, to give it the emphasis it deserves, what has already been mentioned, that:

◆ to be *proactive* implies having the power and ability to choose our responses in any situation or relationships;

◆ to be *creative* implies the ability to generate different possible responses.

The interesting thing to note, and what is generally overlooked, is the fact that real creativity, in this sense, can never happen unless you 'pass through' the proactive level of 'acceptance'. Before you can alter anything in your mind, you have to first 'accept' it (without resistance, being 'neutral') and then alter it. One of the characteristic in the human psyche, which is also often overlooked, is that whatever you resist, persists.

To clarify this further, let us continue with the car analogy. Every car has a gearbox. Gears are provided to enable us to adjust the power of the engine and the speed of the car to suit the external road conditions. While driving a car, if you want to shift the gear to another position, you have to pass through the neutral! Once you are in the 'neutral' (proactive), you can only then go to any other gear-position of your choice – you cannot directly go to any other gear position. It is the same case with our 'response-ability' in dealing with relationships in a proactive and creative way – to develop win–win relationships, especially in people relationships.

In other words, to enable us to choose our response with the appropriate 'power' in any interactions, instead of reacting to anything, we need to first 'accept' with a neutral attitude, a proactive neutrality, whatever is our initial experience in that interaction. Functioning from such proactive state, which is beyond any reactive compulsions, we experience the power of choosing our response.

WIN–WIN RELATIONSHIPS

In relationships, especially human relationships, and particularly in case of conflict, the ideal thing to aim for is to cultivate a win–win resolution, a creative synergy, not just a 'halfway' compromise.

In relationships, especially human relationships, and particularly in case of conflict, the ideal thing to aim for is to cultivate a win–win resolution.

The common approach to conflict resolution has been one of compromise 'in-between' the opposing interests or viewpoints. While this is better than continuation of the conflict, this usually results in a 'win–lose' or even a 'lose–lose' settlement: both the parties may be left with a tinge of dissatisfaction that they had to give up something. Compromise therefore often results in balancing evenly of dissatisfaction! And such settlements, whether intra-personal, interpersonal, or inter-group, are quite often not real solutions of the basic issues in conflict – frequently they are ad-hoc patching up or a forced-fit, and therefore are often neither satisfying nor durable.

The more authentic and effective approach, that of synthesizing and synergizing – the win–win approach – involves enlarging the context of any conflict, rising above the surface or visible issues, and generating a deeper understanding and aligning of the opposing interests through exploring the possibilities of creating a shared vision. This may not always be possible, and it is of course more difficult especially if the issues have strong emotional overtones; but believe it or not, it can be done more often than one may expect. And it is much more satisfying and durable. Even the effort and the process of creating a shared vision generates a positive force and relationship.

Underlying most conflicts in people interactions is the interplay of attitudes.

Underlying most conflicts in people interactions is the interplay of attitudes. If one can identify and deal with the intentions and attitudes of the parties concerned, one could have a better grounding for generating an authentic shared vision, on the basis of which a win–win conflict resolution could be achieved. A few examples of the basic conflicting attitudes are given below in Fig. 3.1.

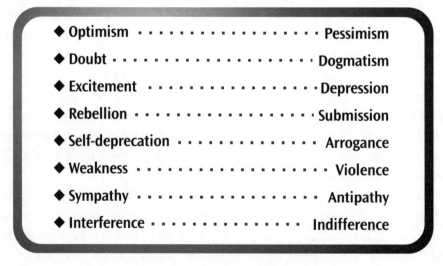

Fig. 3.1 Conflicting attitudes.

The usual approach is to find a compromise somewhere midway between, say, sympathy and antipathy or between interference and indifference. The desirable approach would be to take a more detached overview of the conflicting issues, a kind of helicopter view of the situation, and getting an insight about the real source of the conflict – what is it that each party really wants, irrespective of what is the stated 'upfront' demand. The process of cultivating an authentic shared vision facilitates integrating the intentions and wishes of the opposing parties and reaching a win–win resolution.

A few examples are shown in Fig. 3.2. In all these examples, the point is that instead of pursuing the usual approach of finding an acceptable compromise, the search should be to 'get above' the opposites of sympathy and antipathy, excitement and depression, blind optimism and fearful pessimism, or rebellion and submission, and attempt a synthesis and synergy of benevolent understanding, serenity, clear vision of reality and transcendent acceptance, respectively.

The emphasis is on going beyond the surface issues and sensitizing all the parties concerned, to rise above their narrow self-centered positions and reach a higher level of perception, that of the shared vision, and hopefully achieve a synergy. From this perspective, everyone sharing the vision would be functioning from the 'same side of the table' as it were, instead of from opposite sides. The attitudes and relationships that would emerge as a result would be of interdependence and mutuality, preconditions of a win–win conflict resolution – a basis for healthy and harmonious, authentic and durable relationships.

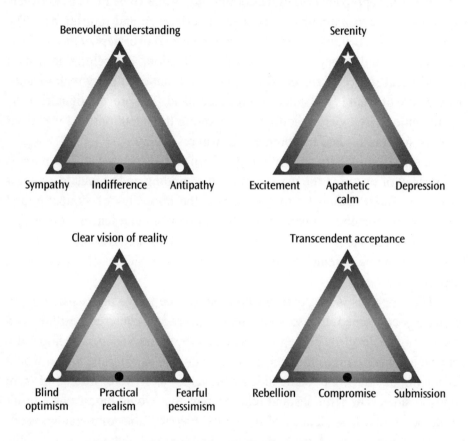

Fig. 3.2   Win–win conflict resolution.

PERCEPTION, CONNECTION, APPLICATION

Let us now consider our basic relationship with life itself. What is life? While life is composed of relationships, it is lived as experience. We have already seen that life is experience and experience is not what happens to you, but it is what you *think* happens to you. And that depends upon your general thinking as to what is happening, what is reality. And this ultimately depends upon your level of perception, or shall we say your 'lenses' of perception.

Experience is not what happens to you, but what you think happens to you.

If the lenses or glasses I wear are pink, then everything I see out there will appear pink to me. If I look at a white wall through such pink lenses, I will perceive it as pink; and if I want it white and even if I keep painting it white, as long as my perception is through the pink lenses, I will perceive the wall only as being pink.

All our relationships, our connections we make in our life with people, things, events and ideas, will therefore depend upon the 'colour' of our lenses or the 'filters' through which we perceive them. The next question, then, would be 'what determines the colour of our lenses – our filters?' It is the level of our consciousness, our self-identity, which will determine not only our perceptions and the connections we make, but also how we 'apply' them in our actual behavior. If the filter is our ego sense, then all our relationships will be contaminated by the self-centeredness of our ego. If, however, we keep our identity with our real 'I', and not the 'me', as discussed in depth earlier, our life experience, our relationships, our perceptions, connections and applications will be at a proactive and creative level.

This brings us to considering our relationships with the issues at the basic existential level – and this would be primarily at the dimension of ideas. While obviously there would be several issues at this level, the main issues, as mentioned earlier, are: *freedom, isolation, death,* and *meaning and purpose of life*.

◆ **Freedom**. One's idea about the concept of 'freedom' would be largely influenced by the kind of early life influences and education one has received. As most of the contemporary education is largely about external phenomena, generally, when one thinks about 'freedom' one tends to imply 'freedom from' something out there, or 'freedom towards' something external – relating to the idea of freedom as if it is an external phenomenon. However, at the existential level, the essence of the concept of freedom, *real freedom*, implies 'internal' freedom – freedom from the ego-sense, the inner relationship, detachment from the ego and the involvement with the proactive inner Self.

◆ **Isolation**. Every one of us has come into this world alone, and will leave it alone. In between these two total isolations, there are many moments of loneliness, feeling utterly alone, loneliness 'in the crowd', loneliness 'at the top', etc. Many people feel uncomfortable with such 'isolations'. If we develop our relationship with our inner Self and identify our existence at this level of consciousness, we will always feel 'connected' and 'related' with everything and everyone around us. There would not be any loneliness, only relationships.

◆ **Death**. This is the only certainty all of us have in life – a non-changeable gravity. And yet, intelligent as we may be, most of us do not like to think about it, much less to talk about it, and even less to plan or live our lives in the context of death, with a proper understanding of our relationship with death.

In fact, most of us have a deep fear of death and 'die' a little death every time we think about it! In order to experience the real power of being alive, we must define and refine our relationship with death.

There are many concepts and belief systems about death. At one end of the spectrum of various beliefs, most people believe that death is a terminal point in our lives. The inner dialogue would be 'I die but the world goes on' and there is sadness and depression, and death is mourned.

At the other end of the spectrum, some people believe that death is not a terminal point, but a transformational stage. What dies is 'me' not 'I' – my ego-self, my body dies. There is a continuity in another 'form'. It is a new beginning. What the caterpillar calls death, we describe it as a butterfly. At the human level, we do not die, we only change our 'cosmic address'! In this case, the inner dialogue would be 'The world dies, but I go on', and death is celebrated.

At the human level, we do not die, we only change our 'cosmic address'!

There are also several other belief systems about death in between theses extremes. One has to choose whatever belief one finds most suitable or acceptable and relate to death accordingly. One thing is certain though. Whatever way we relate to death, we can never prevent or avoid death by worrying about it. In fact if we worry about it too much, we may even invite it earlier! To repeat what has already been stated, we can and should try to do all that is necessary to postpone death and make it as painless as possible, by living appropriately: proactively and creatively – making a life while making a living.

◆ **Meaning**. None of us were consulted, before we arrived on this planet, as to whether we want to arrive on this planet at this time or not! We just arrived and 'graced' the planet one fine day! And no one has really explained to us 'why' are we here in this life. Or what difference would it make to the 'universe', if any, if we were not here. Science and technology has explained a lot of phenomena but has not yet explained to us the meaning and purpose of life.

Of course there are several philosophies and religions, ideas and 'stories' about this, and one has to choose from among these. Earlier, whatever choice one made, one related to and followed that path with much more faith than most people are able to do today, as a result of the advances in modern education and scientific thinking. Consequently, today, especially among younger people, there is a conspicuous lack of any strong internal 'faith' or external 'anchor'. And this seems to have resulted in the weakening, or even sometimes absence, of any strong or deep relationship, with any ideas about the meaning and purpose of life.

There seems, therefore, generally to be a noticeable weakening of commitment to any specific existential idea or sense of belonging to any ideology, or institution, or perhaps even religion, or a clear value system. Overall relationships therefore do become weaker, and this generates a tendency towards superficiality in life – a kind of meaninglessness.

To understand these most fundamental issues of relationships, and to overcome this growing apathy for deeper relationships, especially among the younger population, we need to consider the basic perceptions and visions of reality.

A QUANTUM LEAP TO A NEW VISION

As mentioned in Part One, in terms of physics there are two different views of the universe: the Cartesian–Newtonian model and the Quantum Relativistic model. Let us revisit these concepts, at a deeper level.

The former, based on classical physics, describes the universe as a gigantic super-machine governed by a linear chain of causes and effects. It is a complex mechanical system of interacting discrete particles and separate objects and the basic building block is the atom, which is solid matter – and all atoms are separate.

Moreover, according to this view, the universe exists objectively in a form that a human observer can perceive and measure. It is also described as a mechanistic and deterministic model of the universe, like a clock. It considers matter as solid, inert, passive and unconscious.

It also believes in a dichotomy of mind and matter. Space is three dimensional and homogeneous. Time is unidimensional and linear, moving sequentially from past to present to future.

That kind of thinking has led to analytical, mechanistic, deterministic and reductionist thinking, generating the notion of separateness.

In the quantum view of subatomic physics, quantum mechanics: when you split the atom, you find electrons, protons, neutrons; when you split them you find quarks; when you split them you find strings; when you split them you find superstrings. Beyond that, at our present state of knowledge, you find only a complex web of relationships or energy fields or waves, or energy patterns. In this view, the whole universe is interconnected.

You can perceive reality either as consisting of particles or of waves.

This quantum relativistic model therefore describes the universe as a complex and hierarchical web of inter-relationships. The fundamental building blocks are subatomic particles and levels of energy (quanta), exhibiting the alternative qualities of matter or energy, depending on how they are perceived.

You can perceive reality either as consisting of particles or of waves (wavicles). Light can be perceived as particle or wave. Various objects that you see around you could therefore be perceived as formations of particles/matter or of an interconnected web of energy patterns. In this model, the world of substance is replaced by that of process or relationships. In other words, the universe is perceived as a thought system rather than as a machine. Is a rainbow an object?

The world of substance is replaced by that of process or relationships.

It exists only because of the unique space–time contextual relationships of the rain, the sun and you. In this sense, you create or facilitate the rainbow.

So at one level, things are separate. But at a deeper level, they are connected. To take a very simplistic example, the fingers of our hand appear to be separate from each other if viewed from a certain level. But if we extend our view to a deeper level and are able to see the whole hand, we will find that in reality the fingers are all connected and all of them arise from, and are part of, the same source.

To take another analogy to help clarify this concept: if we look at the various lamps that may be fixed in a room, on the ceiling and walls, we will notice that all of them are separate entities having separate 'bodies', wattages, filaments, may be different colours and so on. But when they are lit, is the electricity, or energy, that they are manifesting different? Again, it is the same source and in a sense all the lamps are linked, interrelated, at the source.

In this systemic world view, we see ourselves as a complex web of relationships or patterns. These relationships extend outwards from ourselves to include other people and ultimately the whole of humanity and our environment. Ultimate reality is a complex web of interrelationships and energy fields. But there is also the surface level: particles/matter perceivable by the human senses. Reality can be perceived at both levels.

Therefore, on the basis of the Cartesian mechanistic view, you would see yourself as a skin-encapsulated entity, consisting of skeletal, muscular, neurological and other subsystems. On the basis of the quantum view of reality, you would see yourself as a complex web of inter-relationships, energy or wave patterns or simply as some kind of order or consciousness.

THE METAPHOR OF THE RIVER

In other words, to understand, manage, and deepen our relationships both within our inner dynamics as well as with the outer dynamics of people, things, events, and ideas, we need to keep in mind a simple metaphor, that of a river.

We, and our life, are like a river: A river is the surface water as well as the land contours of the banks and the deep structures below. You can never step in the same flowing river twice. Similarly we cannot see ourselves twice as we really are. We too are constantly changing, evolving. Moreover, the river can never keep the same landscapes around it until it ultimately merges into the ocean. Similarly, we can never have the same circumstances or relationships around us constantly. Therefore, in terms of managing and deepening our relationships we have to be alive and alert about the constant changes within ourselves and around us. This is the essence of the dynamics of relationships.

If we wish to change the direction and flow of the water of the river, we need to change the land contours, the deep structures below. The flow, the behavior, of the surface water is entirely dependent on these deep structures.

Similarly, if we wish to make a difference in our lives, in our relationships, in our behavior, we need to focus on, and alter, our 'deep structures', our inner driving forces. These can be uncovered, 'dis-covered', and managed, through higher level of consciousness, through detached involvement as described earlier. Trying to change our behavior and deepen our relationships without changing our deep structures, our self identity, will neither be authentic nor durable.

If you want to change what you do, you have to change what you are!

Trying to do more of the same at the surface level, or even better within the same, and expect to make a difference in our relationships, is considered by psychologists as a form of insanity! If you find yourself in a hole, the least you can do is to stop digging! If you want to change what you do, you have to change what you are!

To make a difference we have to become the difference!

Become the change you wish to create.